Cancer

22 June – 22 July

First published in Great Britain 2009
by Harlequin Mills & Boon Limited,
Eton House, 18-24 Paradise Road, Richmond, Surrey TW9 1SR

Copyright © Dadhichi Toth 2008 & 2009

ISBN: 978 0 263 87067 1

Typeset at Midland Typesetters Australia

Harlequin Mills & Boon policy is to use papers that are
natural, renewable and recyclable products and made from
wood grown in sustainable forests. The logging and
manufacturing processes conform to the legal environmental
regulations of the country of origin.

Printed and bound in Spain
by Litografia Rosés S.A., Barcelona

About
Dadhichi

Dadhichi is one of Australia's foremost astrologers. He has the ability to draw from complex astrological theory to provide clear, easily understandable advice and insights for people who want to know what their future might hold.

In the 26 years that Dadhichi has been practising astrology, face reading and other esoteric studies, he has conducted over 9,500 consultations. His clients include celebrities, political and diplomatic figures, and media and corporate identities from all over the world.

Dadhichi's unique blend of astrology and face reading helps people fulfil their true potential. His extensive experience practising western astrology is complemented by his research into the theory and practice of eastern systems of astrology.

Dadhichi features in numerous newspapers and magazines and he also appears regularly on many of Australia's leading television and radio networks, where many of his political and worldwide forecasts have proved uncannily accurate.

His website www.astrology.com.au is now one of the top ten online Australian lifestyle sites and, in conjunction with www.facereader.com, www.soulconnector.com and www.psychjuice.com, they attract over half a million visitors monthly. The websites offer a wide variety of features, helpful information and personal services.

Dedicated to The Light of Intuition
Sri V. Krishnaswamy—mentor and friend
With thanks to Julie, Joram, Isaac and Janelle

Welcome from
Dadhichi

Dear Friend,

Welcome! It's great to have you here, reading your horoscope, trying to learn more about yourself and what's in store for you in 2010.

I visited Mexico a while ago and stumbled upon the Mayan prophecies for 2012, which, they say, is the year when the longstanding calendar we use in the western world supposedly stops! If taken literally, some people could indeed believe that 'the end of the world is near'. However, I see it differently.

Yes, it might seem as though the world is getting harder and harder to deal with, especially when fear enters our lives. But, I believe that 'the end' indicated by these Mayan prophecies has more to do with the end that will create new beginnings for our societies, more to do with making changes to our material view of life and some necessary adjustments for the human race to progress and prosper in future. So let's get one thing straight: you and I will both be around after 2012, reading our 2013 horoscopes!

My prediction and advice centres around keeping a cool mind and not reacting to the fear that could overtake us. Of course, this isn't easy, especially when media messages might increase our anxiety about such things as the impacts of global warming or the scarcity of fossil fuels.

I want you to understand that it is certainly important to be aware and play your part in making the world a better place; however, the best and surest way to support global goals is to help yourself first. Let me explain. If everyone focused just a little more on improving *themselves* rather than just pointing their finger to criticise others, it would result in a dramatic change and improvement; not just globally, but societally. And, of course, you mustn't forget what a positive impact this would have on your personal relationships as well.

Astrology focuses on self-awareness; your own insights into your personality, thinking processes and relationships. This is why this small book you have in your hand doesn't only concentrate on what is going to happen, but more importantly how you can *make* things happen positively through being your best.

I have always said that there are two types of people: puppets and actors. The first simply react to each outside stimulus and are therefore slaves of their environment, and even of their own minds and emotions. They are puppets in the hands of karma. The other group I call actors. Although they can't control what happens to them all the time, either, they are better able to adapt and gain something purposeful in their lives. They are in no way victims of circumstance.

I hope you will use what is said in the following pages to become the master of your destiny, and not rely on the predictions that are given as mere fate but as valuable guidelines to use intelligently when life presents you with its certain challenges.

Neither the outside world, nor the ups and downs that occur in your life, should affect your innermost spirituality and self-confidence. Take control: look beyond your current challenges and use them as the building blocks of experience to create success and fulfilment in the coming year.

I believe you have the power to become great and shine your light for all to see. I hope your 2010 horoscope book will be a helpful guide and inspiration for you.

Warm regards, and may the stars shine brightly for you in 2010!

Your Astrologer,

Dadhichi Toth

Contents

The Cancer
Identity

A smile is the shortest distance between two people.

—Victor Borge

Cancer: A Snapshot

Key Characteristics

Nurturing, sensitive, receptive, flexible, sensual, loyal, intuitive, generous, over-reactive and moody

Compatible Star Signs

Taurus, Virgo, Scorpio, Capricorn, Pisces

Key Life Phrase

I nurture

Life Goals

To be happy emotionally and in family life; to be of service to others

Platinum Assets

Great intuition, adaptability and sincerity

Zodiac Totem

The Crab

Zodiac Symbol

Zodiac Facts

Fourth sign of the zodiac; cardinal, fruitful, feminine, moist

Element

Water

Famous Cancerians

Julius Caesar, Kathy Bates, Mike Tyson, Meryl Streep, Jimmy Smits, Geraldo Rivera, Kevin Bacon, Tom Hanks, 50 Cent, Kathy Bates, Josh Hartnett, David Spade, Robin Williams, Pamela Anderson, Princess Diana, Jerry Hall, Giorgio Armani, Dalai Lama, George W. Bush, Harrison Ford, Nelson Mandela, Carlos Santana

Cancer: Your profile

If you're seeking the most sensitive sign of the zodiac, Cancer would have to top the list. This is not always evident because there are different types of Cancerians. The average Cancerian has the reputation for being emotional, but some born under your star sign, whose totem is the crab, likewise possess hard exteriors and don't often reveal what they're feeling. This can sometimes make Cancer misunderstood by others.

Generally, being born under the sign of Cancer is a wonderful karmic blessing. For the most part, you extend yourself in your caring attitude and always do your best to help others. This compassionate element of your nature is the epitome of what Cancer stands for.

Along with your sensitivity comes an in-built intuition, which is a key characteristic of all of the water signs. You're able to see things others can't see and don't necessarily give preference to your intellect. This will hold you in good stead because you have the ability to sort out the genuine from the fake.

Cancer is an adaptable sign as well. You have the ability to mould yourself to the circumstance. You accommodate others easily and, even though you have a strong mind, you don't necessarily try to prove this at each and every opportunity. You work best in a supportive role with others. Keeping the peace is important to you.

The sign of Cancer is not wishy-washy like water, however. Your personality is quite vibrant at times, and once you get to know others, you're more than happy to share your opinion on a multitude of topics.

Your selfless and nurturing ways draw people to you and you're always ready, willing and able to help others when they need a hand.

Yours is the fourth sign of the zodiac and this relates primarily to home and hearth. This is the mothering zone of the zodiac, so it will come as no surprise that you are a person committed first and foremost to family. This is where you really 'feel at home', especially if you are a woman born under this sign. You try to make your living situation comfortable, and even those who aren't part of your family will always fit in because you take the time to make them feel part of the clan.

This caring, nurturing element of your personality extends to all areas of your life, not just your family. Your key life phrase 'I nurture' demonstrates this. You're the type of person who likes to take an idea from inception and water it with love and attention until it grows into something substantial. This is your way and sometimes others perceive you as being a little too smothering in this respect. But you'll never be accused of ignoring others or cutting corners. Attention to detail and meticulousness are parts of your nature.

Your intuitive capacity is a double-edged sword, however. You know how people feel and in a good situation tend to take on board those feelings very strongly. Of course, if people are in a light-hearted and good mood, you will feel good in yourself. But the reverse is true, too. If you're surrounded by people who are negative, you will tend to take on those qualities as well. It's very important for you to protect yourself and not allow others to dictate your state of mind.

Cancer is ruled by the Moon, a relatively new celestial body. We have observed the fluctuating phases of the Moon and, in the same way as it changes through its varied phases, so too is your Cancerian personality awash with a kaleidoscope of varying emotions. Others will be challenged by these incredible mood swings and, although your family and friends appreciate your kind and warm ways, they are often treading on eggshells in anticipation of that next 'bad mood'.

And, speaking of the Moon, many born under Cancer feel the night is the most invigorating time of the day, so to speak. Just as the Moon comes out at night, you're energised by the twilight hours and will do most of your best creative work in the wee hours of the morning.

Many who are ruled by the Moon have extraordinarily imaginative minds and can create wonderful works of art, compose music and also express their feelings through the written word. If you haven't yet explored these avenues, I strongly recommend you give them a try. You'd be surprised at what will be revealed once you delve into the rich imagination of your inner self.

The other creative area that Cancer excels at is cooking and the culinary arts. Because this so adequately reflects your desire to care for others, it's a perfect amalgamation of your creative skills and your loving personality. With great abandon, you'll whip up the most amazing meals and, coupled with your social skills, it is another aspect of life you should definitely contemplate exploring.

Three classes of Cancer

If you're a Cancer who is born between the 22nd of June and the 3rd of July, the lunar vibrations were very strong at the time you were born. You are primarily emotional and sensitive. Romance, love and married life is the perfect reflection of who you are. Try to keep your emotions on an even keel.

Those of you under Cancer who were born between the 4th and the 13th of July are very focused individuals and this can make you possessive and domineering of your loved ones. In fact, you demand so much loyalty that this possessiveness may drive away the ones you love most.

If you were born between the 14th and the 23rd of July, you are particularly spiritual and selfless in the way you live your life. A bit more practicality wouldn't hurt and this would then help balance your compassionate but often otherworldly attitude. You'll always be surrounded by friends and family because you are an easy target for help. You tend to give too much of yourself to the wrong people.

Cancer role model: Tom Hanks

Tom Hanks' early childhood reflects the changeability of Cancer. He was continually changing schools, religions and stepmothers, would you believe. His adaptability was obviously born and bred in this early home environment. That he is a sensitive individual is shown by his success as an actor and his ability to take on roles just as easily as water takes on the shape of the vessel into which it is poured.

Cancer: The light side

Being with others and caring for them comes so naturally to you, Cancer. This is what attracts others to you. And it is not pretence; you genuinely feel the love you express for all and sundry. Your responsive and perceptive nature is a perfect complement to your generosity. You intuitively understand the needs of others and respond in a way that is in keeping with what they require in life.

Some people take advantage of your goodwill. You must use that perception of yours to discriminate between those worthy or unworthy of the beauty, love and resources you have to offer. Put your intuition into good use.

One area that is not often clearly understood about Cancer is the depth of wisdom they have. You absorb experiences from life and, although you enjoy watching television and reading books, most of your insights are gained through the 'book of life'; what you've personally experienced along the way. This makes you a great teacher and role model to your family, children and anyone else who is blessed enough to have you as a part of their life.

Cancer: The shadow side

Don't let black emotions and negative thinking drag you down into the dark. Cancerian emotions can sometimes be a bottomless pit. Once you dive into that, it's pretty hard to swim back out. You must keep your perspective light and, of course, never associate with others who might trigger any negative, self-destructive emotions.

You have a tendency to brood. You take people's comments way too personally when usually the conversation is general and not intended to hurt you. But still you take it to heart and this is one aspect of your personality that needs to change, especially if you'd like to be happier in life.

Being born under the sign of Cancer also makes you a sensualist. In other words, you like the finer things in life, including sensual experiences, food and drink. However, try not to go to excess because doing this might impact on your health.

Cancer woman

The typical Cancer woman is naturally attractive. This goes without saying because the Moon—which rules those born under your sign—is one of the 'feminine planets' of the zodiac. Your personality is vivacious, sensual and totally alluring to those around you.

Part of your magnetic appeal is the fact that when people first meet you, they don't quite know what you're thinking. Your eyes reflect a multitude of emotions swirling around in that mind and heart of yours. Initially your withdrawn, perhaps shy stance is a contradiction to them. You are graceful, enticing and imaginative.

The popularity you experience is not only based upon superficial beauty, however. People sense that you have a deeper perception of the world and an uncanny ability to understand them, even if they don't necessarily reveal too much of themselves to you. You have a genuine interest in others, so human psychology is part and parcel of your personality. You'd be surprised to find out just how many people hold you in high esteem, even though you may not be aware of it, for the simple fact that you do naturally try to understand them.

You're not in a rush to achieve your professional or personal objectives. You'd rather wait until the time is right to settle for what will make you a fulfilled human being. The other reason for this is that, to you, motherhood and family life are uncompromising ideals. You put them above all other aspirations in your search for happiness and spiritual satisfaction.

Never mistrust your intuition, Cancer, for it will be correct 99 per cent of the time. Your hunches will be right on the money when meeting new people. And, if you get a sense that something is not right, you'll smile later on when you realise you were correct in your assessment.

As mentioned earlier in the book, there are several different types of Cancer. Carlos Santana is the outgoing, creative musician who developed a unique style that has gone down in the annals of musical history. Princess Diana expressed her warmth, sensitivity and creativity in a different way but later on took on the role of advocate for millions of helpless and disadvantaged people around the globe. Whatever category you fall under, the recurring theme seems to be one of nurturing and caring for others, uplifting them and gaining great joy through the process.

In my many years of experience dealing with people, when I've asked a Cancerian the question, 'what do you want most in life?', I've learned there is a common answer. The answer is invariably, 'a family life in which I can do my duty as a faithful wife and loving and dedicated mother'. And often, when marriage comes around, the Cancerian woman is exactly that—the ideal home-maker. You must never make excuses for the fact that you prefer to be a stay-at-home mum. This is an honourable profession and the world, in this rough and turbulent time, needs more women like you who are prepared to stand up, be counted and to take on this most important role.

One of your important karmic lessons in life will be to love and let go. Because you tend to generate so much interest in what you love, you are likely to become possessive and find it difficult to move on in life, especially when it comes to children. Give people space, even though this is difficult, and you'll be richly rewarded for doing so.

Cancer man

A Cancer man is a typical 'sensitive new age guy'. But that doesn't take away from your masculinity. You're certainly more sensitive than the average bloke, but you're fortunate in being able to have the best of both worlds. Those who know you attest to the fact that you can be rash, masculine and at the same time sensitive, caring and loving. This highlights the feminine streak that is ingrained into your Cancerian temperament.

If you've got any doubts about that, take a look at some powerful celebrities, including Harrison

Ford, Nelson Mandela and George W. Bush. No one could argue that these men aren't tough; but at the same time, they are deeply sensitive. Of course, such sensitivity is more quickly and readily noticeable in someone like the Dalai Lama, Carlos Santana or Tom Hanks.

And let's not forget the man of steel, Mike Tyson. If you study his life story you'll see that although he's found himself on the wrong side of the track at times, that sensitive Cancerian element is still very much a part of who he is.

As a man born under Cancer, your powerful receptivity to everything around you is probably the main reason why you are so interesting yourself. Those who have the ability to listen, to take in facts and figures and the experiences of others usually do, after some time, have a lot more to say. And in your case, this does fascinate people.

The Cancer man is an eclectic individual who enjoys all sorts of music, all sorts of literature, and takes a little bit of pride in this aspect of themselves, too. Although a feeling sign, the Cancer man is quite intellectual as well. If you get him on a good day, the Cancerian male is an exceptional conversationalist.

Try not to be too soft on others because there will be moments in your life where you'll be severely let down after giving to someone out of trust, only to find your loyalty betrayed. This, too, will help you grow and give you an even deeper insight into others.

You like to do things properly, personally and professionally. You're methodical and painstaking in your attention to detail. There are some Cancerian men who do climb the ladder of success, but as I said earlier, this is only secondary to their personal aspirations. Your ethics are also of a very high standard and your partners will appreciate this in you.

As much as you give, you expect the same in return. Loyalty and earnestness in your relationships are the cornerstones of what make you a loveable person but also someone who demands the same high levels in return.

Cancer child

If you have a child born under Cancer, you know exactly what I mean when I say that these warm bundles of joy are almost irresistible to cuddle and nurture. They won't have to say anything; they'll just look in your direction and you'll melt. Such is the Cancerian magnetism, which attracts as much love as it gives.

Yes, the child of Cancer is loving to a fault. At times they're a little insecure and need an extra dose of affection and attention to let them know that it's all okay and that there's nothing to worry about. If you're able to do that, you'll set up a great foundation for a well-integrated human being later on. If, however, you withdraw this affection from your Cancer child, you'll be setting yourself up for some complicated emotional issues down the track.

Love and warmth is the dual fuel that powers the Cancerian child's persona.

Your Cancer child is probably moody from time to time and, if you notice they're withholding their feelings, the quickest way to sort this out is to talk to them. Even if they're belligerent and throw tantrums, the fact that you're showing you care will usually settle them down rather quickly. You should never react too strongly because they are excellent mimics and quickly learn what they see. You are the mirror of their future development.

Cancer children have extraordinary imaginations and are curious about life and how everything works. An excellent way to help them develop into well-rounded human beings is to encourage gently their interest in art, music and any other creative activity. They will take to these hobbies like ducks to water. You too will find yourself exploring your own creativity through your continued association with your Cancerian child.

Watery places will of course be some of their favourite hangouts. Taking them to the beach on picnics, ponds, lagoons and rivers are perfect environments to calm their internal emotional turbulence. Teach them how to swim at an early age and you'll probably find they will excel in water sports. This is a superb way to help them channel their volatile emotions.

Because the young Cancerian is changeable, moody and restless, you may need to help them get into a disciplined pattern of study and schooling. Don't let this slide or it could present you with major problems when they move into their teenage years.

Romance, love and marriage

Aloof, cool and distant individuals who are not tactile and demonstrative in their feelings need not apply for a relationship with Cancer. If you happen to be reading this and you fall under that category, you've chosen the wrong person to love.

I say this because Cancer is one of the most loving and demonstrative of the zodiac signs. Cancer dominates the area of family and domestic affairs and this is at the forefront of their mind in any relationship they enter into, even if they don't openly acknowledge it.

Casual affairs are not generally the domain of Cancer. Being born under this sign, you are primarily interested in a committed and long-term deal. To you, marriage, the time-honoured institution, is sacrosanct and taken very seriously. To you, there is nothing worse than a failed marriage or broken family life.

The lucky partner who has you as their mate on the journey through life is indeed fortunate. You'll shower them with affection and genuine love. This is not just lip service. Because you have a touch of Scorpio in you (being one of the other water signs of the zodiac), you are intense in the way you love. You can even be possessive and jealous at times, but you justify this because you give so much in your relationship that you expect the same in return.

You have a powerfully intuitive nature and connect with others immediately without any thinking process involved. If that happens and you feel that you've met your soulmate, you're probably right. You won't need anyone—friend or relative— to endorse your feelings. You trust this inner part of your nature and this is probably the best way for you to travel when we speak of Cancer and love. Rely on your own discretion and feelings as to the suitability of your partner.

This intuitive aspect of your nature is also very unsettling to others on first meeting you. You have a remarkable ability to know what they're thinking or about to say before they do. This makes it almost impossible for your friends to tell you fibs, because you catch them out before even they know they've been caught out!

If and when you find a partner who will love you with the same tenderness and passion that you do them, you will give your all. You firmly believe in a relationship of equality and mutual respect. Unfortunately, some Cancerians tend to give more than they receive and then find it difficult to change the ways of their partners. You know what I'm talking about when I refer to this personality flaw of yours.

When you become aware this is happening, you need to nip it in the bud early. The only way you'll gain respect is by drawing a line in the sand and saying to your partner 'enough is enough'. Your fear of rejection or the possibility of losing someone you love from being a little too firm with them is unfounded. Speak your mind and do so by being quietly assertive. This will work wonders and set your relationship aright.

Yes, your partner or spouse does indeed have their work cut out for them with you. They're constantly on their toes, trying to figure out in which direction your emotions are moving. You are extremely changeable and in some ways you like this because it makes life so much more interesting for you. But remember: others may not be quite so enamoured by such a fluctuating state of affairs and may even tire of it.

Don't jeopardise your relationship by assuming that others enjoy your unpredictability as much as you do. On the other hand, you may not be able to control these feelings and that's where more open dialogue will be necessary. Don't let shyness impact upon your social success. Less outgoing Cancerians need to develop their social skills more and not hide from the world. Practice makes perfect!

You are loyal and faithful as a friend and as a lover, and these are great traits for attracting an excellent partner into your life.

Health, wellbeing and diet

It's now a well-known medical fact that one's physical health is a mirror of one's emotions. In saying this, you, Cancer, probably need to take note of it more than any other sign of the zodiac because your feelings dominate your life so very strongly.

When you have a thought or a feeling, an associated chemical and hormonal reaction takes place, which impacts upon you physically. Positive thoughts and feelings result in positive chemical and wholesome physical states of being. Negative thoughts and/or emotional feelings have negative ramifications for your physical wellbeing.

I'm driving this point home because this would have to be the single most important factor influencing your health and ultimately your longevity. Spend time each day working on clarifying your feelings and removing those thoughts that will drag you down.

On the physical level, Cancer rules the chest, stomach and breasts. You are constitutionally weak in these areas and, when things go wrong, here is where you may suffer.

Some Cancerians also suffer from asthma and bronchial disorders; but this again may have to do with suppressed childhood issues that need to be released so these problems can clear up.

I mentioned earlier your love of the sensual aspects of life, including eating, which means you are possibly prone to overeating. In this respect, try to moderate your diet and don't mix too many different food types. Because you are a water sign, you probably also like to drink a lot with your meals; not just alcohol but even water. However, liquids dilute the gastric juices and can cause fermentation, bloating and other digestive disturbances. Wait some time after eating before taking a drink and, although this may be difficult at first, you'll soon get the hang of it.

Fruits such as honeydew melons, bananas and other lighter-coloured fruits and vegetables are excellent tonics and pick ups for your body.

Vegetables including squash and potatoes are also good for your star sign, but eat these in moderation because they are higher carbohydrate foods. Finally, low-fat cottage cheese, cucumbers, lettuce and other salads are great for your metabolism as long as you eat small portions several times a day. Chamomile tea is great for calming your intense mood swings.

Work

Unless you absolutely love what you do in your work, you'll be destined to be miserable, Cancer. One of the key issues in your life—in everything you do, including your work—is the level of love and attention you feel comes from your actions.

For this reason, choose a line of work that affords you the opportunity to work closely with others in a role where your feelings can be given adequate room to develop and be shared.

You're very responsible, dependable and extremely punctual in the way you conduct yourself and so you can expect to go far professionally.

Many born under Cancer develop a hobby at home and finally grow it to a fully-fledged business. Be patient because you may have to do this on a part-time basis until the profits start to make it viable.

Money is important to you only because it offers you stability and roundedness. In the professional arena, however, you can use money as a means of developing your career interests and so banking, real estate and other financial institutional professions would ideally suit you. Nursing, counselling or welfare work and other associated medical fields, as well as cooking, catering and hospitality industry work will also give you a high sense of satisfaction.

Key to karma, spirituality and emotional balance

Believe it or not, the sign of Pisces is strongly linked to some of your most important life lessons. Think about that for a moment: Pisces is the most selfless of the zodiac signs and so this should immediately ring a bell when you realise just how caring and loving you are to others. Your compassionate and universal love for the world is part of your nature, which reflects this Piscean attribute.

The key words 'I nurture' will be the basis for the way you live this life. And this underpins your need for warmth, love and security. Remember that giving is as important as taking for the simple reason that great joy and satisfaction are felt by those who are doing the giving.

Mondays and days of the new and full Moons are exceptionally good days to develop your spiritual inclinations. Meditation, prayer and other spiritual practices that can help you develop your powers of intuition and psychic abilities will be accelerated on these days. Moonstone, pearl and white colours can also be of use in this respect.

Your lucky days

Your luckiest days are Mondays, Tuesdays, Thursdays and Sundays.

Your lucky numbers

Remember that the forecasts given later in the book will help you optimise your chances of winning. Your lucky numbers are:

2, 11, 20, 29, 38, 47

9, 18, 27, 36, 45, 54

3, 12, 21, 30, 48, 57

Your destiny years

Your most important years are 2, 11, 20, 29, 38, 47, 56, 74 and 83.

Star Sign
Compatibility

Take calculated risks—that is quite different from being rash.

—George S. Patton

Romantic compatibility

How compatible are you with your current partner, lover or friend? Did you know that astrology can reveal a whole new level of understanding between people simply by looking at their star sign and that of their partner? In this chapter I'd like to share some special insights that will help you better appreciate your strengths and challenges using Sun sign compatibility.

The Sun reflects your drive, willpower and personality. The essential qualities of two star signs blend like two pure colours, producing an entirely new colour. Relationships, similarly, produce their own emotional colours when two people interact. The following is a general guide to your romantic prospects with others and how, by knowing the astrological 'colour' of each other, the art of love can help you create a masterpiece.

When reading the following I ask you to remember that no two star signs are ever *totally* incompatible. With effort and compromise, even the most 'diffi-cult' astrological matches can work. Don't close your mind to the full range of life's possibilities! Learning about each other and ourselves is the most important facet of astrology.

Quick-reference guide: Horoscope compatibility between signs (percentage)

	Aries	Taurus	Gemini	Cancer	Leo	Virgo	Libra	Scorpio	Sagittarius	Capricorn	Aquarius	Pisces
Aries	60	65	65	65	90	45	70	80	90	50	55	65
Taurus	70	70	70	80	70	90	75	85	50	95	80	85
Gemini	70	70	75	60	80	75	90	60	75	50	90	50
Cancer	65	80	60	75	70	75	60	95	55	45	70	90
Leo	90	70	80	70	85	75	65	75	95	45	70	75
Virgo	45	90	75	75	75	70	80	85	70	95	50	70
Libra	70	75	90	60	65	80	80	85	80	85	95	50
Scorpio	80	85	60	95	75	85	85	90	80	65	60	95
Sagittarius	90	50	75	55	95	70	80	85	85	55	60	75
Capricorn	50	95	50	45	45	95	85	65	55	85	70	85
Aquarius	55	80	90	70	70	50	95	60	60	70	80	55
Pisces	65	85	50	90	75	70	50	95	75	85	55	80

Each star sign combination is followed by the elements of those star signs and the result of their combining. For instance, Aries is a fire sign and Aquarius is an air sign and this combination produces a lot of 'hot air'. Air feeds fire and fire warms air. In fact, fire requires air. However, not all air and fire combinations work. I have included information about the different birth periods within each star sign and this will throw even more light on your prospects for a fulfilling love life with any star sign you choose.

Good luck in your search for love, and may the stars shine upon you in 2010!

Compatibility quick-reference guide

Each of the twelve star signs has a greater or lesser affinity with one another. The quick-reference guide will show you who's hot and who's not so hot as far as your relationships are concerned.

CANCER + ARIES
Water + Fire = Steam

You'd have to be considered brave to enter into a relationship with the fiery Aries. This is not what we would consider the best match in the zodiac, but the fact that Aries is passionate and hot-tempered is in itself something that may be alluring to you. You will rise to the occasion and enjoy the challenge of being with your Aries suitor.

Aries have zest, a love of life and, if you can keep your moods under control, this relationship does have a chance of going to the next level. The elements of water and fire, which rule each of your signs respectively, are quite opposite in nature, but Aries does warm the cockles of your heart and stimulate your deeper emotions. You in exchange have the ability to calm the turbulent energies of your Arian friend.

Because of your sensitive and deep-feeling nature, you might find Aries a little superficial at first. You need to be prepared to take them to a deeper emotional place—perhaps a place they haven't been to before. This will be your primary challenge in a relationship with them.

There are some good financial indicators for a match between Cancer and Aries as well. There's a good balance when it comes to combining your resources—your attributes being nurturing, whereas Aries is pushy and industrious. You'll find elements in each other that support and help you to grow emotionally, materially and spiritually.

Your sexual relationship will be an interesting one. You are quite at variance with each other with your sensitive and touchy nature requiring a little more softness than the abrupt and brash Aries is able to give it. No 'wham, bam, thank you ma'am' type of treatment for Cancer, thank you, but unfortunately some Aries are like this. As a result, your feelings are likely to be hurt by this rather quick and insensitive approach of Aries.

Those Aries born between the 21st and the 30th of March are not particularly suited to you as lovers but you can both become good friends and have much to talk about, particularly spiritually or philosophically.

Getting together with those born between the 31st of March and the 10th of April will suit you well as long as money is at the top of your agenda. This is a good business arrangement but not necessarily the best of romantic combinations. An Aries born during this period will help you grow your financial security and personal status. In some ways, you are karmically destined to be together.

Those Aries born between the 11th and the 20th of April are a rather tough group to deal with and you'll be tested on many levels. Such Aries need to be loose and fancy free, so they won't necessarily satisfy your need for someone who is family orientated. These Aries have a strong sense of self and are sometimes selfish in their attitudes. Along with that, they are quite independent and it might be hard tying them down to a long-term and committed relationship.

CANCER + TAURUS
Water + Earth = Mud

Cancer and Taurus can enjoy a lifestyle that encompasses both the financial and the emotional aspects of security. One thing, however, is that you might find Taurus a little too preoccupied with the material concerns of life. But you have to give this to them: they will look after your needs and are extremely loyal. You can relate to these characteristics.

Because of your rather intense and volatile mood swings, you probably need someone like Taurus to help stabilise your feelings. They do have a tendency to make you feel more grounded and in control of yourself.

Female Taureans can themselves be a little moody so that's one area that may be a problem, especially if you try to obstruct them or disagree with the way they like things done. Give them enough space and they'll love you for it. Let them do things their way on their terms and the relationship will prosper and grow very quickly.

There's a great meeting point for both Taurus and Cancer in the family arena. This is the single most important common interest you both share. Taurus is also not that proud where it comes to getting down and helping out in the family, doing chores around the house and taking pride in the way your home and family environment looks.

Your domestic and financial security is vouchsafed by your involvement with Taurus. They are hard workers and you admire this quality in them. You'll be satisfied by their desire to please you and make sure that all your creature comforts are tended to. They're not particularly impromptu or improvisational and need a strong routine to live by.

If you hitch yourself to a Taurus born between the 21st and the 29th of April, you may find yourselves passionately involved at the outset, only to find the gloss wearing off in time. This is because astrologically you are not all that well suited. The communication between you is a little lacklustre and unless you can work on ways to open your hearts to each other, this relationship may not go too much further.

If you choose to become involved with a Taurus born between the 30th of April and the 10th of May, you will be extremely pleased by their wonderful sense of humour. Keeping their company will stimulate you and a great social life together is indicated. You will draw many friends into your orb of influence and this should be a reasonably fulfilling relationship for both of you.

Taurean individuals born between the 11th and the 21st of May are rather materialistic and overly concerned by money at times. This could get up your nose and, although you are quite amenable to the idea of having a good lifestyle, their obsession with money and possibly even their penny-pinching ways will not sit well with you.

CANCER + GEMINI
Water + Air = Rain

You experience life primarily through your feelings. However, Gemini is often out of touch with that part of their personality, relying mainly on their thinking and deductive processes. As a result, communicating with them can become rather frustrating, and vice versa. Your tendency is to measure things by asking, 'how do you feel about that?' And in contrast, Gemini will ask, 'what do you think about that?'

There are some similarities that can cement your love but you both need to work hard at them. With Gemini, so intellectually engaged and often scattered in their approach to life, you'll need to express your patience to an even greater degree than you usually do. You are enamoured by their intellectual skill and diverse abilities, especially in the way they express their feelings, but they also tend to be proud intellectually and this may ultimately affect your self-esteem.

Using your psychic abilities may be another way you can bridge the gap between you and your Gemini partner. Being psychic is not necessarily intellectual but you have that uncanny ability to grasp what another person is thinking without even talking about it. Gemini will be amazed at this.

Sexually speaking, there is an attraction between you and Gemini and the two of you can enjoy many hours of frivolous fun together if you both let down your guard. Humour and laughter is the antidote to many of the challenges that a Cancer–Gemini relationship can encounter. Make it the basis of your relationship and your sexual lives will grow in proportion to the amount of laughter you have.

You'll be at odds in the way you want to handle your money with a Gemini born between the 22nd of

May and the 1st of June. The differences are rather marked. Try to clear this up at the outset of the relationship so that you don't end up bickering about who owes what and who should take responsibility for which bills. This will be the major issue in a relationship with a Gemini born in this period of time.

For the Gemini born between the 2nd and the 12th of June, you'll have great fun with them and, socially speaking, will never be bored. They have the strong influence of the happy and sensually attractive Venus. You'll be very attracted to these Gemini-born folk and their sensual magnetism will make it hard for you to avoid a relationship with them. You can combine your ambitions and make a go of it together materially as well.

You're sexually attracted to any Gemini born between the 13th and the 21st of June but you mustn't overlook the fact that there's more to a relationship than just these sexual energies. Do you want a deep and abiding commitment from your Gemini partner? That could be a little difficult for these individuals because they're scattered in so many different directions at once. This could undermine your stability and security at the end of the day.

CANCER + CANCER
Water + Water = Deluge

You feel an instinctive connection with any other Cancer due to the fact that your sensitive and intuitive personalities see so much of yourselves in each other. That's a great start. But is it enough?

You both generally aspire to the same things in life and on a day-to-day basis feel comfortable in each other's company. Without even saying too much, you both move in the same direction pretty much at the same time. Your temperaments are very well suited. Family life and, in particular, your love of children and working in a domestic sphere will be very harmonious.

You're both dominated by your feelings and this, on a bad day, will definitely be a problem for both of you. As long as one of you is not experiencing a deep and sullen Cancerian mood, the other will be able to cope and lift you out of those negative feelings. If, however, you are both going through one of those intense mood swings, you'd better stay out of each other's way. It could be like a massive rain cloud descending upon the Cancer family.

If you decide to consolidate your relationship and spend a long time together, it's not a bad idea to have a game plan. This is important with Cancer because you're so prone to letting your emotions determine what and how you want to do things that you may run off the rails.

Sexuality is important for both of you as Cancer-born individuals; mainly because you see it as a way of expressing what you feel for each other emotionally. When a Cancer loves another person, they want to demonstrate this in many, many ways. As long as you feel secure and care about your Cancer partner, you'll experience the heights of bliss in the bedroom together.

If you finally settle down with your Cancer partner, expect to hang out together enjoying cooking, gardening and other house chores. Just the fact that you're in each other's company won't bother you so much, even if the chores are quite tedious. Being home-bound is not a big deal for you both because this is the primary domain of Cancer.

Sexuality is particularly important to a Cancer born between 22nd of June and the 3rd of July. You'll need to be prepared to offer them lots of physical gratification if you become involved with them. This is in part due to the Scorpio influence on these individuals. These Cancerians are very powerful emotionally and may want to dominate you as well.

If you choose to fall in love with any Cancer born between the 4th and the 13th of July, you can expect this to be a good combination and you'll also feel satisfied sexually with them.

You have some incredible karmic connections with other Cancers born between the 14th and the 23rd of July. This combination promises a good destiny. Because the Moon is exceedingly strong in its influence on you, you may need to make an extra effort to control your feelings and not react too strongly to each other. Try not to be possessive of each other's time, either.

CANCER + LEO
Water + Fire = Steam

Your Leo partner is proud, egotistical and dramatic in every respect. You must never give them a reason to feel embarrassed. They are particularly proud of the partners they choose in life and, if you happen to be the fortunate one that Leo has chosen, you'll need to be on your best behaviour and also able to satisfy their large egos.

Leos can be very demanding of your time. If you have a career of your own and a full diary, this might start to create tension for you in your relationship. Don't expect the proud Leo to make as many concessions as you do. Being naturally a giver, you will be the one who has to succumb to their demands and eventually may start to resent it.

Leo can be a lot of fun and this is one aspect of their personality you absolutely adore. They are definitely the life of the party and once you're infected by their love of life, it might be a little difficult to break from the addiction of a relationship with Leo. Wherever they go, they shine their light and the response they receive will spill over to you. You'll enjoy adulation and, at times, even being in the limelight with them.

There's an unusual balancing act that occurs with Cancer and Leo. This is to do with the elements ruling you. The hot-headed and fiery Leo is calmed by the soft, watery element of Cancer and Cancer is warmed by the fire of Leo. This bodes well for the relationship, but Leo must soften their approach while you must learn to stand on your own two feet independently of Leo.

If you involve yourself with Leos born between the 24th of July and the 4th of August, there's a strong financial association with them. They are your 'lucky rabbit's foot', if I can put it that way. They tend to bring you increased financial welfare and your energies seem to function well together. This is a great combination if you're both ideally attracted to making money.

With Leos born between the 5th and the 14th of August, the planet Jupiter dominates them, along with the Sun. You could feel a little overpowered by them, too, in that they can overstep the boundaries of your comfort zones. They are ambitious to say the least, and to your way of thinking, this is risky and jeopardises your sense of security.

Primarily, Leos born between the 15th and 23rd of August are your best match. You could possibly meet these people through some professional or study activity. However, there may be some hidden or clandestine influences associated with this relationship. In any case, there's a lot of passion and intense emotional activity associated with your relationship.

CANCER + VIRGO
Water + Earth = Mud

You're quite in tune with people's personalities and it would be a big mistake for you to overlook the contradictions you initially find when you come in contact with a Virgo. Trust your intuition if you fall in love with them but don't do so too soon. You need to work through some of the differences between your and their personality.

A relationship with Virgo may not go to plan. Although you are both feminine elements of the zodiac and can find compatibility in many areas, the most important shortcoming for you is the critical attitude of Virgo.

Always ready to find fault and to indicate where something can be done better, this will most certainly wound your sensitive nature. Out of courtesy, you may not say anything initially but how long can you let that build up for, Cancer? No, it's best for you to respond in the first instance so that Virgo understands clearly that constructive criticism is quite okay by you but there are ways and means of expressing those criticisms.

Both of you are quite imaginative but you work primarily through the faculty of feeling, whereas Virgo is an intellectual/earthy type. You might find it hard to reconcile the endless schemes and methodologies of Virgo when to you, if something feels right, you should just do it. That will annoy Virgo and here again we see the basic differences between your personalities and how that might adversely impact upon a long-term relationship for you.

When it comes to lovemaking, you might be quite surprised at the rather straightforward, clinical approach a Virgo takes to the process. They may bypass the whole level of feeling that you're so accustomed to. You believe in romance and wooing one another in the game of love. The straightforward, clinical approach is not for you. So here, too, we see the difficulty in satisfying yourself with a Virgo partner.

Communications can run into difficulties with Virgos born between the 24th of August and the 2nd of September. Virgos are normally chatterboxes but this group may not necessarily be so. You'll have to delve a little deeper to find out what these individuals are really like. You'll feel confident, however, once you scratch the surface a little more and see that practically there's more to them than first meets the eye.

You could find yourself a reasonably good marriage prospect in a Virgo born between the 3rd and the 12th of September. The two of you will connect quite quickly and develop some strong emotional and sexual bonds. Don't move too quickly, though. Be patient, hang in there, or you're likely to miss some of the more tender qualities of these Virgos.

Great friends can be found in Virgos born between the 13th and the 23rd of September. You need to get ready for some high-class social action by connecting with them. They have a great all-round knowledge and this will keep you interested and entertained in many areas of your life.

CANCER + LIBRA
Water + Air = Rain

This is a challenging relationship, to say the least. Libra seeks freedom at all costs, being an air sign. You'll be prepared to give them some latitude in this respect but may not receive the commitment that is so very necessary in the Cancerian scheme of life.

The significant differences can be summed up fairly simply in the fact that you need a quiet and retiring type of domestic environment, whereas Libra likes the lighter side of life, including social, playful and variety-seeking activities. Of course, this is not to say you don't want to participate in these activities and will usually shine as much as your Libran partner does. The problem is one of protracted fun with a lack of commitment to the more serious side of life as you need it.

On a sexual and intimate note, Libra is rather flirtatious, unlike you. This could give rise to jealousy and possessiveness on your part, especially if you perceive their social antics as dismissing you or somehow demeaning your self-worth. You'll need to talk about these things because this is another area that just seems to be ingrained into the Libran nature. Fun and social interaction to them is synonymous with flirting.

You need to address any issue with Libra quickly as it arises. By holding back you're likely to react and say things to hurt them. Unfortunately, although

Libra doesn't seem to be quite as sensitive as you, they are in fact quite prone to feeling battered, especially when you're in one of your moods. Don't beat around the bush with them and your honesty will help patch up these differences that are being discussed here.

You get on well with Librans born between the 24th of September and the 3rd of October. A great sense of mateship can be found with them and you'll support each other with good advice. They have an interesting view of life and you'll learn much from them. Just keep an open mind.

Librans born between the 4th and the 13th of October tend to rile you up. They are likely to be rather blunt in the way they express themselves, which will cause a fierce reaction in you. These Librans can be very demanding and emotionally draining as a result. Notwithstanding this, the sexual attraction between the two of you is strong.

You must tread carefully with Librans born between the 14th and the 23rd of October. There could be problems financially and your loans, borrowings and other financial arrangements will create uncertainty if not conflict. Librans are a changeable type of person so their decision making is not often their best character trait. You may need to take the lead in this area to avoid any financial messes.

CANCER + SCORPIO
Water + Water = Deluge

Even in your first encounter, you will wonder how it's possible that you could feel so comfortable with a stranger so quickly. This is the mystery of the elemental interactions of the zodiac. Scorpio is as sensitive, emotional and caring as Cancer, but also very intense in their expression of these emotions. Along with their kind and loving ways, there is the demanding and often sarcastic element underlying their emotions. You will need to adjust yourself to the mysterious and powerful Scorpio moods.

One thing you are attracted to in Scorpio is their ability to communicate their thoughts and their feelings and also their intentions through the mechanism of their eyes. The reason you like this is because you believe that when two people fall in love, they should somehow be in tune and understand what each other thinks and feels without necessarily speaking. You'll have this in full measure with your Scorpio partner.

Scorpio is a sexual dynamo and few star signs are capable of keeping up with this high level of demand. The other water signs such as Cancer and Pisces are able to do so, which is another reason your compatibility rating is so high.

Scorpio's possessive, jealous and often vengeful attitude on the one hand can make you feel so loved yet on the other create many difficulties for you as well, particularly if you are a social type of Cancerian.

Scorpio demands consistent and persistent acknowl-edgement of them and reassurances of your love. This can become rather tiring day in and day out, but the fact that they express these feelings is your guar-antee that they definitely love you.

Scorpio will dominate your domestic and social environment so you'll need to toughen up and take a stand to regain position in the scheme of things. As far as the pecking order is concerned, Scorpio likes to be at the top and this may make you feel down-trodden at times. You need to assert yourself more.

With a Scorpio born between the 24th of October and the 2nd of November, you'll have instant and permanent attraction. You'll become aware of their sexual appetites very quickly and will enjoy the attention that they shower upon you. This is a fine combination and you'll instinctively feel connected and easy with each other.

A spiritual connection is likely if you are attracted to Scorpios born between the 3rd and the 12th of November. Both of you have a lot of knowledge to share but you particularly are able to impart some deeper insights to your Scorpio partner. In this rela-tionship you will experience mutual respect.

Your emotional rapport with Scorpios born between the 13th and the 22nd of November is very powerful. At times, Scorpio, the silent sign of the zodiac, may find it hard expressing the depth and variety of their feelings but you'll easily be able to do this in your relationship with them. The two of you have the ability to work and grow together.

CANCER + SAGITTARIUS

Water + Fire = Steam

The Sagittarian character is strangely an attractive one to you but this is not a combination you should quickly enter into without serious thought. You are attracted to them because of their easygoing personality. If you feel shy and apprehensive in the company of others, let Sagittarius show you how it's done.

Your Sagittarian partner is loved by everyone without exception. Generous to a fault, you admire this magnanimous trait on their part and wish you could do it as lavishly as they do. But this relationship may not work and one of the important reasons for this is your changeable moods. Once Sagittarius gets a taste of your unexpected emotional fluctuations, they'll be walking in the opposite direction before you've finished your next sentence.

You tend to retain thoughts, events and memories of the past and to you, the way Sagittarius just glides over these issues is rather fascinating. You wonder how they do it. You can't quite get your mind around how they don't get bogged down in this head space. You approach these life issues and relationships in a very different way. Sagittarius has a philosophical view of things.

Sagittarius is very blunt in what he or she has to say and so you'd better toughen up if you want them to give you the truth, the whole truth and nothing but the truth. You may think you want the truth, but as Jack Nicholson yelled to Tom Cruise in the movie *A Few Good Men*, 'You can't handle the truth!' Don't ask for straightforward honesty from your Sagittarian partner because they'll give it to you, and it won't be giftwrapped, either.

Cancer and Sagittarius do have some sexual attraction to each other but it may not last long. You are softer and more sensitive in your approach to lovemaking, compared to the larger-than-life 'give it to me now' Sagittarian. Sagittarians see sex as a form of conquest and love to satisfy their sexual and physical needs. You may not be satisfied emotionally by their responses to you.

With Sagittarians born between the 23rd of November and the 1st of December, you'll make good friends with them but may also be confused as to what they want in the longer term. You could be lured by the hot, sexual, seductiveness of the moment with them but, when all is said and done, you'll realise that this is not a particularly strong match that will remain satisfying to you.

Sagittarians born between the 2nd and the 11th of December are a really good match for you because there's a high degree of compatibility; marriage is likely with them. Unlike most Sagittarians, this group is an exception. You'll feel drawn to their vision, their enterprise and the fact that they're able to think independently of the masses.

You have a great connection with Sagittarians born between the 12th and the 22nd of December. You're also financially compatible with them. An attraction to their personality is there but the focus will most certainly be on your financial connection together.

CANCER + CAPRICORN

Water + Earth = Mud

You mustn't think for a minute that just because your Capricorn partner is at times a little serious and introverted that he or she doesn't fully identify and appreciate what you are feeling. You'll soon come to understand that Capricorn, your diametric opposite in the zodiac is, in a lot of ways, quite well suited to you even though they're not that good at expressing their feelings.

One thing with Capricorn you have to accept at the very outset is their need for financial security and material welfare. They do tend to equate who they are with what they have. This is very different to the way you perceive life, so you'll somehow need to combine their materialistic ambitions with your intuitive need for a happy life.

Capricorns definitely like what money can buy, so in one sense this works in your favour because, of course, having money to supply the needs of your family, your children and friends is definitely a bonus, especially if you can do it in full measure. In other words, your association with a Capricorn will never see you want for anything. In fact, they like the most up-to-date things, even if they are a little frugal in the way they spend their money.

Don't expect Capricorn to be overly communicative but you'll always be supported by them and they are intensely loyal individuals. Rest assured that, if you have a problem, you can rely on them and they'll always be there to back you up.

Sexually and emotionally, your signs seem to be at odds with each other. Sensitive and emotional Cancer needs more than the restrained affection that Capricorn offers. It's not that they won't share themselves sexually or physically, but they may not know exactly how to do it. Cancer to the rescue! Show them how it's done.

Marriage and permanent bonds in a relationship are quite likely with those born between the 23rd of December and the 1st of January. You really feel a kinship with these individuals. This very strong attraction between you is likely to develop very quickly. On occasion, the Capricorn individual you are attracted to during this period may be quite a bit older than yourself. You may need to deal with the social stigma attached to this.

With Capricorns born between the 2nd and the 10th of January you can expect a really great relationship. They'll fulfil most of your dreams. And, you could have a great physical and sexual relationship with them as well. Now that has to be a bonus! They stimulate your imagination sensually and creatively. It also seems that art and culture will be an important component of your relationship with them.

There's great sexual chemistry with Capricorns born between the 11th and the 20th of January; but, this could remain only a superficial relationship. Take the time to help these Capricorns develop more of a connection with their own emotional selves as this will in turn help forge a better relationship between the two of you.

CANCER + AQUARIUS
Water + Air = Rain

Unfortunately, love catches us off guard at times, doesn't it, Cancer? And, with Aquarius, ruled by the sudden and impacting Uranus, this may be one relationship which does exactly that. You may not see the Aquarius coming and, before you know it, you're involved in a deep and intense relationship with them.

It would serve you well to contemplate where this relationship will go because Cancer and Aquarius are very different breeds of people. You're pretty much a homebody, while the Aquarian is out and about, interested in social and political affairs.

Aquarius is an air sign so they live primarily in their heads, in the realms of ideas and concepts. It's hard for them to connect with the emotional side of their nature and for this reason they will appear aloof and distant, sometimes appearing to love in a world of their own. You, with your changeable emotional states, and them with their often wilful, unstable routine, is not exactly the best combination for a stable family life, is it? Aquarius will leave you up in the air about where you stand, even though you may already be completely besotted by them.

If your Aquarian partner can settle down just long enough to let your lunar vibrations touch their soul, they may finally make contact with their deeper feelings. But this might be a pipedream, like wishing for humans to make contact with extraterrestrial life. We all believe it can happen but to date it just hasn't.

Your sexual relationship together is likely to be passionate and, irrespective of the age of the Aquarian, there's always a bit of 'hippie' in them. They hang loose and like to play the field. That's not going to sit too well with you. They are very progressive in many ways and in particular sexually.

With Aquarians born between the 21st and the 30th of January, you can expect a challenging time. They could leave you exhausted and desperate for attention and affection. To them, the mental banter and intellectual exchanges they perform should somehow satisfy you on every level, but that's not what you feel.

The schedule of Aquarians born between the 31st of January and the 8th of February is wild, hectic and unpredictable. That could frazzle your nerves, to say the least. If you yourself are a person who is constantly on the go and involved with considerable travel, perhaps with your work, then you might enjoy combining your schedule with them and the rollercoaster ride that will ensue.

You can safely fall in love with Aquarians born between the 9th and the 19th of February. There's great friendship and sexual attraction between the two of you. Their crazy antics will humour and inspire you in a weird and wonderful way. You find them different but not different enough to make you feel concern that they can't provide you with your basic needs in life.

CANCER + PISCES
Water + Water = Deluge

A match between Cancer and Pisces is one of the few ideal combinations of the zodiac. The great news is that you instinctively feel at peace with each other. Your emotional connection is strong and this is probably the strength and foundation of a relationship together.

Even if Cancer and Pisces disagree, as is likely in any relationship, you're able to settle down quickly into a comfortable and relaxed state of affairs again. And interestingly, although Cancer is known to hold onto their feelings, to develop grudges, that may be difficult for you to do with Pisces. Why? They just have a way of helping you release these feelings.

Pisces is the most selfless sign of the zodiac. You thought you were a giver! Wait till your Pisces partner pampers you with universal love and their divine radiations of compassionate care. You'll feel as if you are in heaven. It's true that Pisces aspires to giving of themselves and often do so to their own disadvantage. As long as they're supplying you with all your needs in this selfless manner, you'll be happy. But, what would happen if you realise that it's equally important for them to share this love on a universal level with everybody?

Sexually, your intimate moments will border on the fantastic. There is a religious undertone to your sexual relationship. When you make love with your Pisces partner, you will forget everything and experience a whole new dimension to your being. This will be pretty irresistible for you and something you'll find extremely difficult to break away from if, for some reason, the relationship bogs down in other areas of your life.

Deep, spiritual ties are evident with Pisces born between the 20th and the 28th or 29th of February. These are some of the most idealistic Pisces, whose vision for a utopian lifestyle might find difficulty reconciling with the reality of life on a practical level. They will need you to help them in this respect. In doing so, don't crush their ambitions but gently lead them to a state of practical and spiritual balance.

The best match is most likely with Pisces born between the 1st and the 10th of March. They have a strong, compassionate and empathetic nature that you admire, and this will draw you closer together over time. This is an excellent love and sexual combination. These individuals have the strong influence of the Moon, which is your own ruling planet. You'll see yourself mirrored in them and because of this, they are able to accommodate you easily and fulfil each and every one of your needs.

The key words in your relationship with Pisces born between the 11th and the 20th of March are sexual power and attraction. The dominant theme of this group of people is magnetic control, mainly because Scorpio has a strong influence over them. If you open yourself up to an individual born during this period, you will be completely engulfed by the relationship. There'll be no turning back. You'll feel apprehensive in your initial connection with them but will learn to grow into this extraordinary relationship. Eventually, you'll feel blessed and fulfilled by having opened up to their power.

2010:
The Year Ahead

We are still masters of our fate. We are still captains of our souls.

—Winston Churchill

Romance and friendship

The year 2010 is an excellent one for those of you born under Cancer. With Jupiter making a lucky aspect to your Sun sign, this is a year when fortune smiles upon you and love and romance take on a greater significance in your life. You'll be able to promote your ideas and be fortunate to associate with people who can open many doors for you. Introductions to prospective partners will be numerous, especially in the early part of the year with Venus, the Sun and Pluto transiting your zone of relationships and marriage.

Relationship problems that might have plagued you over the previous months are likely to disappear, so look forward to a brand new cycle where you can focus on what you really want in life. This is the time to assert yourself and attract the type of person you feel you deserve.

In January, when Jupiter moves through your zone of philosophy and higher learning, you will be particularly interested in using your good fortune for the development of others. You will see life in a completely different light and will apply these new insights to your relationships.

At this time travel and interest in other cultures will also occupy your mind and many born under

Cancer will choose to take a journey, connect with friends and family, or even start planning a move that they believe will make them feel more comfortable about themselves. If previously you have had reservations about your ability to attract others, then in 2010 your views about them and your life and work in general will be different.

During February and March, Mars will activate your physical energies and you will want to imprint your ego on everything you do and anyone you meet. You will have much more drive to achieve your romantic ambitions and will be very effective in expressing your personality. You will feel much more independent and less reliant on others. Some of you already in relationships will see this is a time to assert yourselves and take over the reins of leadership in your marriage or long-term relationships, whereby in the past you may have been subservient and frustrated that your partner has been dictating the terms of the game.

This is a time of great freedom as shown by the influence of the independent and progressive planet Uranus in the upper part of your horoscope. In March and April you have the green light to try something different, to meet new people and go out on a limb to explore the different aspects of your personality and social life that you otherwise wouldn't normally attempt.

You are likely to meet extremely interesting people at this time. You also feel comfortable about unwinding, relaxing and simply being yourself. You may be using these energies to break free of limitations but that may also create some tension. Be careful in your choice of relationships and don't do things that will embarrass you or damage your reputation, even if it's fun at the time.

One of the difficult planetary combinations for you this year is the placement of Saturn in your zone of inner happiness and family life. This forecasts a big step in your spiritual and personal evolution and it may not be easy to deal with. In April you may start to feel the pinch of the planet considered to be your karmic tester. Your relationships might cool down a little and you'll be forced to reappraise the value of your friendships as well.

Big changes are likely at this time if you're prepared to take the steps to make your life better. You may even choose to renovate your appearance, much to the amazement of your family and friends.

Unforeseen changes in your relationships will continue between May and September. Try to look at this as a reflection of your own patterns of behaviour and the need to grow. Pluto, the planet of transformation and rebirth, associates with your karmic planets in your marital sector. 'Death' of sorts should take place now and you will be 'resurrected' in your view of what a relationship is really all about.

Mars makes you more vocal in the way you express your feelings and this may be out of character according to your spouse or lover. Whereas in the past you may have bottled up your feelings, this is a time when you'll be more verbal and prepared to call a spade a spade. Others may not feel all that comfortable with your direct approach at this time.

By the time June comes around, with Venus affecting your Sun sign very powerfully, you're likely to find yourself in the middle of some new romantic opportunities and will feel that you must carefully consider them or you could miss the boat. Those with whom you come in contact may not be the usual sort of people you would dream about or consider your cup of tea. But you'll be surprised at how much more open you are to trying something different. Over and above this, Jupiter will make you more prone to taking risks with others, so be careful that your over optimism doesn't lead you up a blind alley.

Brace yourself in July and August when Mars and Saturn enter into a most difficult transition in your domestic sphere. This could be the time of the year when your patience is most tested. Dealing with relatives and members of your own family could feel like banging your head against a brick wall. Nobody will be listening to you, even though what you have to say makes perfect sense.

Venus takes some of the pressure off in the latter part of August and through September, but this may be cold comfort as you try to deal with your emotions and someone who is less than willing to open up and share the deeper parts of their emotions with you. If this is someone you trust or have a close intimate relationship with, it may be that a disappointment takes place and you begin to see them in a completely different light.

A passionate if not wild cycle can be expected in October with the placement of Venus and Mars in your zone of love affairs. This is an excellent transit for singles who are looking for some excitement and possibly a relationship. I say *possibly* because love affairs have a tendency to be fly-by-night. As long as you're prepared to regard the experiences you have at this time as steps to your deeper wisdom and understanding of others, there should be no problem. This is going to be a rather lusty time for you.

Your confidence will continue to be extremely high, especially in the first week or two of October. In early November, however, you could be rather quarrelsome and may not get on so well with those around you. Mars will create tension and a greater degree of competitiveness with others. You may also feel a touch of envy that other people have what you don't and this could be the cause of you trying to outdo them. Try to remain balanced and appreciative of what you have in life. This is the secret of attracting better things.

During this same interval, the position of the Sun and Saturn again in your zone of family and domestic issues indicates that a greater responsibility may be placed upon your shoulders. Being the caring type, you could well find you need to take over the care or affairs of an older member of the family. Balancing your time and carefully assessing your priorities will be part of this transition in the latter part of 2010.

In November your concern with family will continue; however, there is a shift to the younger people in your life with Venus, the Sun and Mercury transiting your zone of children. This should be a carefree and fun time when you connect well with the younger members of your family or indeed anyone who is junior in age.

You will feel zest for life and a greater creativity through this period because this zone of your horoscope has much to do with creative expression and other recreational and sporting activities. If you're involved in competitive sports, it could be a lucky period and you could combine this with your social life to your own best advantage.

In December, the final month of the year, be careful that you don't embellish your stories or you'll find yourself in hot water. Trying to make an impression on others is one thing but you may get yourself into a spot of bother by not exactly expressing the truth of the situation or the way it is. Others may question your credibility at this time, which could make you defensive. Fortunately, Venus brings with it additional romantic and social opportunities, especially around Christmas time. What an excellent way to finish 2010! Enjoy.

Work and money

You sense that something exciting, something different is about to happen in your professional life and work in 2010. You feel this from the word go and it is due to the extraordinary influence of Uranus edging its way towards your career sector in the first few months of the year. However, it may not be until June that you feel its full impact, and until then, you'll be working on new ways of directing your skills and capitalising on your past knowledge.

In January, use the power of Venus to sway others. Your influence can yield great benefits professionally. Networking will definitely be your strong point and the Sun also makes you extremely popular. Combining your business life with pleasurable and social activities will be a distinct advantage in furthering your career ambitions this year.

In February, Mercury gives you the opportunity to tie down a deal, to get all the fine details sorted out to negotiate a win–win situation with a business partner or an employer. You are aggressive and hungry for extra money, as shown by the placement of Mars in your zone of income throughout January to early July. By all means seek out extra cash and income, but don't let this dominate your personal relationships.

You could find yourself between a rock and a hard place when it comes to making some important decisions about your professional direction in March and April. On the one hand, there is the chance to bathe in some glory by being offered a promotion; but on the other hand, there is the temptation to move on to more exciting avenues of professional expertise. These will be difficult decisions for you but the placement of Saturn in your zone of domestic activity might have the final say. You will need to consult with loved ones before making any firm decision because this will impact on them quite significantly.

Whichever choice you make, the placement of Mercury and the Sun in your zone of profitability throughout May is a great omen that should see you pocketing some increased income through your work or business activities. If you're a home-maker, you might find yourself landed with some extra cash, which will give you the opportunity to splurge on yourself. That's also highlighted by the fact that Venus is strengthening your twelfth zone of expenses and so you spare no cost in finally acquiring those 'islands' that have been on your wish list for some time.

Don't let your emotions get in the way of conducting yourself methodically at work in June. The Moon and Venus make you overly sentimental and cause you to overlook important details. It's not a bad idea to invite the assistance and advice of a co-worker if you feel that you are unable to deal with the fine print of contracts. It would be a shame to sign on the dotted line and later regret the decision. Make sure that what you are committing to doesn't leave you hamstrung with bills further on in time.

The Sun returns to your sign of Cancer in late June and throughout July, so this is a wonderful time to shine in the world. Your popularity will increase and those you work with will look to you for guidance and leadership. It appears you will have the right answers at the right time and will be respected to a greater degree by your employers.

In July and August travel associated with your work may not be all that enjoyable. Your frustration will tell and you mustn't let your power get the better of you at this time. There may be moments where you could abuse your power, taking advantage of others who work under you, which will only compli-cate the situation. Try to be fair in your dealings and physically exercise as much as possible because you will definitely need to let off steam.

Expenses and other activities centred on the home front may blow out throughout Septem-ber and October. You may not realise this until November or December when the bills start pouring in. Your accounting may not be in keeping with the reality of your bank balance. It is particularly impor-tant to assess such information before committing to construction work, renovation, or indeed the purchase of a new home.

As 2010 draws to a close it's likely that your debts may bother you. Knowing this, astrology can give you an insight beforehand so you can take the appropriate measures to remedy the situation. With Christmas and social events pressing hard on you in December, try to live frugally and remember it's the thought that counts, not necessarily how much you spend. By using this approach you can still enjoy spending but will not regret the size of your bills in the new year.

Karma, luck and meditation

Jupiter moves through the luckiest zone of your horoscope during 2010 in the latter part of January. You won't have to make too much of an effort to feel the influence of this benevolent planet, but try to use these gifts wisely.

With power and abundance at your fingertips, there is often a tendency to be wasteful. By using your gifts and opportunities fairly this year, by sharing and caring, you invite even greater luck and fortune into your life.

In March and April, Venus also moves through this lucky zone of your horoscope and this culminates in April with enhanced prestige, increased income and social popularity. You will not only have money but a considerable amount of inner happiness as well.

June and July are months when you carefully take stock of yourself. Life is a balance of your inner and outer selves. Meditative practices and possibly even a spiritual retreat might be appealing at this time. This is an excellent way to rejuvenate yourself, both emotionally and physically.

In July and August your frustration might cause you to overlook an opportunity that is not immediately attractive. Try to look at the big picture, the longer-term benefits of what is offered. They say 'all that glitters is not gold' but in this case the reverse might be true.

In August and September there are distinct

opportunities in your work. You may be opposed by your family and loved ones on a decision you make but stick to your guns and be true to yourself.

There's no harm in reconsidering your choices in the last three months of the year. Don't be afraid to say simply, 'I'm not sure; I need more time'. This will give you the opportunity to make the right decisions and enjoy the wonderful benefits flowing from that.

2010:

Month by Month
Predictions

Time, which changes people, does not alter the image we have of them.

—Marcel Proust

Highlights of the month

January is an extremely busy month and your connection with others will be noticeably stronger than usual. You could expect to be spending loads of time exchanging information with others or gathering data and bits of research material for both work and personal reasons as well.

Between the 1st and the 10th you'll be working through issues on the home front that may not be clear. Dealing with relatives, a sibling or even the birth of a child within the family may create a few days of havoc.

On the 13th when Saturn moves retrograde, your family affairs will again come to the fore. Your efficiency in dealing with information, contracts and other pertinent documentation will be spotlighted and the success or otherwise of the month will hinge largely upon these matters and your abilities.

Heavier responsibilities weigh on your shoulders between the 14th and 16th and the fact that an eclipse of the Sun takes place in your marital sector is most telling on your personal relationships during this phase. A new stage of relating is about to begin where secrets, issues from the past and other events that have been swept under the rug for way too long will be brought back into the open.

Between the 17th and 19th your contractual obligations to the ones you love will be highlighted. Give and take will be the order of the day. You'll find that your charm will not necessarily be enough to convince others of your rights, needs or desires. Negotiation will be an important focus at this time.

Wastefulness and dealing with money and other matters associated with your budget will occupy much of your time on the 20th. Reappraising your work practices will bring you some new information that will help you solve your material and financial dilemmas.

As the Sun enters your zone of shared resources at this time, wills, legacies and other important tax or accounting issues will make you focus on them to the exclusion of everything else.

Between the 21st and the 31st the focus is on work and the Sun produces some excellent results when you'll find success and popularity with your employers and peers. You'll be able to get along with everyone at work and this should be a productive time when the application and appreciation of your talents will raise the bar in your work environment.

You'll be identifying strongly with what you do, so your particular specialised skills can be used with greater effect in the early part of 2010.

Romance and friendship

Between the 1st and the 3rd, your confidence is extremely high and you have the gift of the gab. However, on the 4th, don't assume that others are resonant with what you have to say. Your communications may be in conflict with your own best interests. Others may see you as a braggart rather than someone genuinely trying to share your ideas and feelings.

The period of the 11th till the 13th is excellent for your personal relationships. You are likely to grow closer to others and the eclipse on the 15th highlights this fact. There could be intense feelings of love and a greater need for security. Try to gain a long-term perspective on this otherwise you'll simply be demanding that your short-term needs are met before seeing the whole picture.

Travel plans are spotlighted between the 17th and the 20th. You can broaden your intellectual horizons as well and for many Cancerians this is a time to reconsider going back to school or taking on a home study course.

You'll be in the limelight after the 21st and others will be fascinated by a story you have to tell. This may not be something occurring in the present but a quirky recollection of past events that will surprise even you when they come to mind.

Your social life heats up after the 23rd, with the Moon entering the eleventh zone of friends and partners. Even if you consider yourself a loner of sorts, this is a time when you'll be more prone to connecting with the group mentality and working harder to be accepted among your peers.

A new friendship or alliance is likely to be formed at this time, leading to greater self-confidence around the 27th. Catching up on letter writing or diarising your thoughts and the events of the week will be highlighted around the 31st.

Work and money

Mars is firing you up to earn more, to achieve more and to be seen to be more successful. These feelings could be accentuated between the 2nd and the 10th. You are more emotional about money and acquiring the good things in life, but don't let this blind you to the needs of your family.

On the 15th, a solar eclipse in your zone of public relations and business partnerships high-lights the importance of strengthening your ties with the people that count. You need to re-establish your commitment to others.

For better or worse, your financial obligations and ties to others will come to the fore around the 20th. If there are loose ends you've previously ignored, this is the time to finish them off and move forward.

Get your bets and bills in order between the 25th and the 29th. You could have overlooked the fact that some banks charge late fees if punctuality isn't adhered to. This is a way you can also save money, even if at first it doesn't seem like much. Over the year it could add up to a sizeable amount.

Destiny dates

Positive: 11, 12, 13, 14, 15, 16, 17, 18, 19, 21, 22, 23, 24, 30, 31

Negative: Nil

Mixed: 1, 2, 3, 4, 5, 6, 7, 8, 9, 10, 20, 25, 26, 27, 28, 29

Highlights of the month

Your sexuality and intimate relationships are characterised by a more intellectual and independent way of thinking. After the 2nd you'll be analysing the relationships you have and whether or not the physical aspects are all that satisfying for you.

Due to the placement of the Sun, Venus and Neptune in the most intimate zone of your horoscope, and as well with Mars forming an opposition aspect, much will be hinging on your sexual satisfaction. If you are frustrated in this way at this time, these negative feelings and reactions may spill over into other areas of your life, including your work.

With Mercury in a fluster after the 8th, be careful how you communicate your thoughts and ideas and to whom you communicate them. You may be relying predominantly on your intuition, which is represented by the strong influence of Neptune. Your communications may be very idealistic and, even though you grasp what you're saying, don't assume that others are on the same page. You need to be clearer in expressing your intentions and the meaning of these ideas.

The magnetic quality you exude after the 11th is not solely dependent upon how you look or speak. There is a spiritualised quality to your efforts and an eagerness to understand the meaning of life and your place in it. Jupiter produces some lucky vibrations for you and, with re-entry of Venus into the same sector, some stroke of luck, chance meeting or other avenue for success is opened up to you without you even asking for it. Your aura will be strong and people will gravitate towards you easily.

When Mars creates dynamic aspects to your work sphere between the 26th and 28th, you can expect your physical vitality to wax. The downside of this energy, however, will be to learn that self-mastery can relieve you of an over-inflated ego and tendency to run roughshod over others. Maintaining humility and treating others fairly will be essential in keeping the peace.

One of the key lessons in February is how to redirect your energy. No doubt you'll be able to accomplish many feats in half the time, but you may also have the tendency to abuse the power that you have. Use the extra time you gain wisely.

In this latter part of the month you are also likely to want to take a vacation or at least a short journey to get away from everything. This is a great idea and will further enhance your interest in spirituality, the occult or self-improvement techniques.

Romance and friendship

You'll have a greater desire than usual to understand yourself in relation to others between the
2nd and the 4th. Your domestic interactions will be
more serious. You may be trying to extract information from an older member of the family who's not
saying too much. Perhaps they just need a little
bit of space. Don't push too hard and you'll be
surprised at how much they'll offer to you when not
asked.

On the 9th and 10th, your sexual feelings run
high. By the 11th, this could involve someone at a
distance, or possibly even a telephone affair. Online
dating agencies are also highlighted at this time
and you may find yourself a recipient of many offers,
albeit with those who may seem somewhat strange
and quirky.

You'll be feeling great after the 18th when the
Sun triggers your philosophical and spiritual interests. Try not to be too over the top with friends,
particularly in a social situation where your enthusiasm for your views may not be as strong as theirs is.
However, this enthusiasm does have the potential
to alter your lifestyle.

From the 20th to the 24th, your self-enjoyment
barometer will be raised several notches and you'll
want to party and have fun. Someone you meet at
this time will lift your level of passion as well. Once
you get to know them you may not want to share
them with your usual group of friends for some

reason. You are very territorial about your loved ones.

A restless state of mind characterises the period of the 26th to the 28th. You may have itchy feet and won't be able to keep your mind on what's at hand. You may also retaliate strongly if your partner or spouse starts to enquire nosily into what you consider is your own personal business.

Work and money

Don't assume you've finished all your work this month because Mars moving in its retrograde motion indicates the need to plug up a few holes in your strategy and review what you earlier thought were good decisions. Once you've done that, a few speculative enterprises may start to pay off handsomely, especially after the 4th.

Loaning money to others after the 7th may be unavoidable, especially if they're close friends or family members. This may come upon you suddenly so you may have to drop everything to assist someone in need by handing over a few dollars.

Your accounting practices are again under the spotlight after the 10th, with Mercury entering your eighth zone of joint finances, taxes and accounting. You may be unhappy in the way some of these affairs are being handled, especially if a third party is involved whom you've hired to do the job. It could be that some Cancerians will take back control over these issues.

A legal matter that has to be dealt with should be done after the 14th. 'Fortune favours the brave', so don't be afraid to give your instructions clearly and strongly, otherwise you'll lose respect.

Between the 25th and the 27th, it's best to spend a little more to purchase quality rather than cutting corners to save a few pennies only to find later that what you've purchased is inferior.

Destiny dates

Positive: 3, 4, 11, 18, 20, 21, 22, 23, 24, 26
Negative: 7, 8, 10, 25, 26
Mixed: 2, 27, 28

Highlights of the month

March is an extremely busy time and this is shown by Mercury's entry into your zone of higher education, information and self-improvement. You could expect plenty of phone calls, letters and information changing hands between the 1st and 5th.

With Venus edging close to the unpredictable Uranus, you'll have an optimistic but somewhat erratic approach to your relationships and your life generally. You are particularly attractive between the 6th and 7th and meeting someone who will influence your life at this time is not out of the question. You might even go so far as to try something different like putting your name down at a dating agency or even venturing into online cyber-space to meet someone new.

There could be changes in your business and professional life during this phase as well and, when Venus comes to the position of your career zone around the 8th, some new windows of opportunity will be flung wide open for you to consider. You'll have the chance to set up a Dutch auction between your own employers and those of another company who may desire your services as much, if not more. In short, this gives you a distinct advantage in demanding extra money and respect, if you so choose.

Financial matters that might have been left up in the air due to the retrograde movement of Mars are likely to march forward around the 10th. The important point financially is to take full responsibility for the situation in which you find yourself. Be gracious, even if someone has misled you and you haven't exactly achieved the results you had expected.

You might find yourself interested in astrology, tarot and other psychic sciences, and be drawn to people who have similar interests to you after the 16th, because Mercury influences your Sun sign and the way you think.

Inspiration seems to be very powerful throughout this third month of 2010, and collaborating or writing with others will make you experience a new lease of life. Sending your scripts to publishers or magazine editors will meet with some success.

Lucky vibrations continue throughout the period of the 18th to the 21st, with the Sun further activating your professional arena. Your organisational abilities and your ability to see a project through to the end will attract the interest of your employer. These are the qualities that will single you out from others and give you the chance to earn more money and feel a greater sense of self-worth.

If you are working in the home, family members will have a greater appreciation of what you're doing than usual and will surprisingly pitch in to give you a hand. This will definitely bring a smile to your face.

Through the 21st to the 30th the health or emotional wellbeing of an elder of the family will come to the fore and you may have to spend considerable time helping out with their needs.

Romance and friendship

If you're trying to win friends and the approval of others you must do so in a gracious manner, especially between the 1st and the 6th. No one will be able to argue that your facts or opinion are anything but correct; however, your manner may get people offside.

A lighter, charming energy can be expected around the 8th when Venus climbs to the top of your chart, with some excellent results. Your attractiveness and popularity will be evident to everyone. You'll also want to step out of the usual mould and be different, exciting and possibly may even try to shock some of your loved ones with a whole new approach to your life.

Between the 9th and the 11th, you'll want to try something different by way of mixing with unusual characters who'll keep you on the edge of your seat. You'll be ambitious about pushing the limits; but remember there are consequences if you live too hard and too fast.

You'll have an opportunity to make a mark for yourself with a new social circle after the 20th when the Sun culminates into a new self-understanding. This is more than likely going to be triggered by someone you meet during this cycle who is possibly considerably younger than you are in years.

Seek the advice of a close friend after the 25th. Your mind could be foggy and your decisions may not be based upon the correct criteria or information. Letting your emotions dictate the direction of your life may not be all that good an idea.

On the 31st, a party or group activity will require you to be the central figure in its outcome. The co-operative spirit surrounding you will bring out your character's best 'flavours', so to speak.

Work and money

Mounting pressure and changes in your workplace will actually be a blessing in disguise and will force you to see things more clearly. From the 1st till the 7th, nothing will remain still and you will have to improvise, get on top of your tasks, and understand what's happening in your workplace.

Uranus creates uncertainty, and possibly drastic measures will need to be taken to give you the advantage over others between the 10th and 15th.

By the 17th, you can have communications about, or instigate, some new policies that give you a sense of greater self-determination. Your ideas will be met with a warm reception, even if you at first think it could be an uphill battle convincing others of your views.

Between the 25th and the 29th, you may need to reconsider bank loans and other mortgage repayments to stay abreast of possible interest rate hikes. Re-negotiation is not as daunting as you think: it's simply a matter of asking your bank manager to rework your affairs for a better or fairer deal for yourself and your family.

Destiny dates

Positive: 8, 16, 18, 19, 20, 21, 31
Negative: 12, 13, 14, 15, 25, 26, 27, 28, 29
Mixed: 1, 2, 3, 4, 5, 6, 7, 9, 10, 11

Highlights of the month

Between the 1st and 4th you'll probably find yourself blocked creatively. If you are using the same old worn-out techniques to relate to others, to complete your work or to artistically produce something, you'll find this period challenges you to step outside yourself and try something completely different.

If you *are* having some sort of creative block, try opening up a dictionary and picking any word on the page. Let your mind focus on its meaning. You can also use this as a form of fortune-telling for it is known as 'bibliomancy, a form of divination'. This has an uncanny way of revealing the future or something pertinent to a situation or question you have in mind, as well as opening you up to the spontaneous creativity of the moment. The point I'm making is, you should use alternative techniques to help propel you forward to overcome this temporary feeling of emotional and creative emptiness.

You'll be called upon to do something quite special in April. This is due to the powerful exaltation of the Sun in your career sector. You'll be shining bright among your peers and loved ones. Everyone will be looking to you for leadership, to help steer them in the right direction.

Under these circumstances you must be careful that your expertise and skills are up to the task. Winging it won't work. If you're thrown a task that is beyond your ability, it is better to let your superiors know your limitations rather than trying to pretend you know more than you actually do. Your honesty will be appreciated and this will help keep your integrity intact.

Contracts and other verbal or written agreements need careful attention before the 18th. Mercury will move into its retrograde motion at this time and confusion, half-truths and missing information will make forming decisions arduous tasks, indeed. It is best to wait a while until I indicate to you the better period for signing off on these matters.

The Sun activates friendships between the 20th and 23rd. A new circle of friends is likely to invite you into their orb and this will stimulate you mentally and possibly even excite you physically. The chance to connect with people who have a broader view of life will make you realise how much you have been missing and your eyes will be wide open with the possibilities that are presented to you in this phase of your life.

Relationships could be somewhat confusing after the 25th, when Venus moves into the twelfth zone of secrets. This is also likely to be a time when you could venture into uncharted territories of taboos and socially unacceptable behaviour. Illicit affairs, sexual or other physical cravings or habits may have to be dealt with for you to move to the next stage of your personal evolution.

Overall April will be an interesting month but the position of Venus also shows a great deal of waste and expenditure, which needs to be curtailed.

Romance and friendship

The sense of restriction you might be feeling can be both internal—that is, to do with your own personal happiness—and external, relating to your domestic sphere. This is due to the placement of Saturn in this part of the year. You'll be more sentimental between the 2nd and the 7th and will demand that your personal needs are met. This will be more pronounced if you feel you've been short-changed in a relationship.

April is also a time of love and courtship and, if you're feeling less than rewarded for the efforts you've been putting into your friendships, your desires may manifest in the form of a new lover coming into your life. Between the 14th and the 17th, there is a strong possibility of meeting a soulmate. You're likely to be in the right place at the right time.

Relationships, communications and in particular promises or given pledges may spin out of control around the 18th with Mercury going retrograde.

Hidden feelings or other clandestine events arise after the 25th. You'll be actively engaged in situations that are not visible to others. You may have to work through some past karma and issues to do with lovers, friends or family members with whom you previously have had a falling out.

An on again/off again affair may settle down after the 27th. If earlier you felt as if you were being coerced or taken advantage of, this will change and you'll realise you now have a greater say in the relationship because there is a feeling of mutual equality.

Between the 28th and 30th, you'll follow the crowd only to find yourself landed in a situation that is not at all comfortable. The type of people or company you find yourself with may even make you feel unwell. There's no need to justify your actions if you decide to opt out or leave early.

Work and money

You're on the right side of your boss between the 1st and the 3rd but this may elicit feelings of envy and jealousy from those around you. You're likely to achieve a promotion or improve your salary.

Your concentration levels are great, you'll receive accolades and your sense of self-esteem will be going through the roof.

Your éloquence will help you get out of a tight situation sometime between the 12th and the 15th.

You can see opportunities where others overlook them and, by so doing, you can cement your professional relationships and increase profitability.

Between the 17th and the 20th you have a talent for dealing with the general public and, yet again, the manner in which you speak and the way you present your ideas is appealing to customers and co-workers alike.

There is the capacity to achieve a new job if you so choose. Interviews and discussions after the 23rd are fruitful and some real changes are likely by the 28th if you want them.

On the 29th, mixing with a group of powerful individuals will help you recognise your own abilities and creates potential for future growth in your work.

Destiny dates

Positive: 12, 13, 14, 15, 16, 17, 19, 20, 21, 22, 23

Negative: 4, 5, 6, 7, 25, 30

Mixed: 1, 2, 3, 18, 28, 29

Highlights of the month

This month you could be feeling rather weary due to your involvement with too many people. Balancing work and social commitments will be taxing, especially between the 2nd and the 5th. You have a strong desire to connect with new friends and idealistic people. You'll be clearing out the old to make way for the new and this is the continuing theme for you during 2010; you desperately wish to have a new start in many areas of your life.

Saturn continues its push for you to examine yourself and find new ways of learning about how you can remodel yourself or create a new niche in the world by building a more secure future.

By the 6th your excessive work practices may cause you to feel unwell, frustrated or just generally apathetic about your work and your day-to-day grind. Boredom may set in. The search for the new will be extended to discovering novel ways to keep your mind stimulated and interested.

Part of your frustration might centre around the fact that you realise you need to tighten your belt, financially speaking, but still want to continue to have the social life you desire. When the Sun enters your quiet zone of secrets and behind-the-scenes activities on the 21st, you're likely to pull back and this could send out some mixed signals to those with whom you are normally more communicative. At this time you simply need to explain to them why you are doing what you are doing. Sharing your feelings will work far better for you than locking yourself away and disconnecting from the group.

However, your romantic affairs do pick up by around the 25th when you will appear more charming and refined to others than you usually do. Accept that date, go for a new job, and generally get out and about because this will be a time when you need additional stimulation to get you out of a rather dull mood.

Performing a service or giving a hand to someone you love is also an important activity to help you get out of the rut that you find yourself in this month. By forgetting your own problems and extending kindness to others, you'll feel much better about yourself and also go a long way to improving your relationships, especially on the home front, where Saturn will continue its journey for some time to come. It's best to put on a smile, even if you don't feel all that crash hot. As the old saying goes, 'until you make it, fake it'.

Romance and friendship

Your speech this month is straight to the point and around the 2nd you'll either scare off people or enamour them to make them want to get much closer to you. Use that element of mystery to attract potential partners. By the 4th, you will feel extremely sexual and may be able to enjoy some additional moments of intimacy with the right person.

Expect lots of excitement and enjoyment with friends by the 6th. The Sun and Mercury transiting your eleventh zone of social affairs now give this part of your life a distinct boost. You must, however, be careful not to get embroiled in differences of opinion. This is due to the tension between Mercury and Mars.

Between the 10th and the 15th, there may be several unsettling situations that lead you to believe someone is not being straightforward with you. Lies and deception may be revealed and this could create a great deal of disappointment in someone whom you thought you could trust.

Between the 16th and the 18th, don't be afraid to use your allies, ferret out information and get to the bottom of a situation that is bothering you. Behind-the-scenes activities will yield rich and eye-opening results.

From the 18th till the 21st, you'll need to change your schedule and accommodate the difficulties of a close friend. This may involve some travel and could even cause you a great deal of inconvenience, but unfortunately your sense of obligation may win out against your own needs. But don't worry; you'll be drawn closer in a friendship related to this, so there's always a silver lining to each dark cloud.

On the 23rd, pull together family members for a pow-wow. By the 25th, one of the younger members of your family may need to be reined in. Health matters and dietary issues are strongly highlighted between the 26th and the 29th.

Work and money

Others conveniently forget the fact that they owe you money between the 4th and the 9th. Reminding them may help speed up the return of that money but could also see them retaliate unjustifiably. You have to weigh up the pros and cons between getting your money back and maintaining a friendship. If they're going to react like that, you think to yourself, who needs that kind of friend?

Doubts about a contract clear up between the 11th and the 14th. You'll be more likely to feel comfortable about giving the nod to it at this time. Research your subjects well, study the fine print and sign off so that you can move on to greener pastures.

Profits and possibly a pay increase are likely to appear between the 12th and the 14th.

The Moon activates your income streams between the 18th and the 20th. Don't be emotional about how you spend money. Think carefully about subscribing to something that may be of no use after two months. Being landed with a twelve-month contract for something you don't need will later irritate you.

Speculations pay off on the 25th and the stock market seems to be of greater appeal to you.

Destiny dates

Positive: 16, 17

Negative: 3, 4, 5, 6, 7, 8, 9, 10, 15, 21

Mixed: 2, 11, 12, 13, 14, 18, 19, 20, 23, 25, 26, 27, 28, 29

Highlights of the month

For those Cancerians romantically involved, June can be a time when your love union develops into a future marriage prospect. Your feelings for a loved one are rich, deep and more varied. You'll be better able to see the upside of your personal relationships after the previous difficult month.

Jupiter's transition into your most powerful zone of career will also cast its favourable aspect on your domestic circumstances, producing more pleasant communications and some additional good news thrown in for good measure. It seems that most areas of your life will feel the beneficial influence of Jupiter.

Your energy lifts to a new level after the 7th with Mars entering your zone of courage, communications and mental power. You'll have the capacity to execute your plans with great diligence and physical drive as well. Your sensual nature will be much stronger and people will be enamoured by the high level of energy that you exude.

Try to balance yourself throughout June as this extraordinarily high level of energy may meet with some resistance later in the month or throughout July when Mars comes in touch with Saturn. If you expend too much energy now you won't have any left for the more important work ahead of you.

By all means initiate new projects or ventures this month. Your magnetic charm and industriousness will definitely lay down the perfect foundation for future success.

By the 11th you'll have some great opportunities to connect with people who have similar social and business interests. New commercial partnerships are likely to be formed but they will not be based purely on greed or material acquisition. Feeling empathy for others and vice versa will make you feel comfortable in your working relationships, and this is the time of the year when you can feel truly understood by those you are engaged with professionally.

Life gets better after the 15th with Venus bringing you ample money and further business opportunities. If you've struggled to make ends meet you may be able to loosen the reins of control and have some fun again. Life looks pretty good for you from the 15th till the 21st.

After the 21st the Sun returns to its birth position bringing with it a heightened sense of self-awareness and generally good feelings. You will want to embrace the world and this is marked by popularity and good success.

Some light-hearted fun and also flitting about here and there is forecast for you between the 25th and 28th, when Mercury also injects its dose of humour and frivolity into your heart. The end of the month should be quite a lot of fun and you should take the opportunity to make your presence felt in any social situation to which you are invited.

Romance and friendship

You're influential between the 1st and the 8th, and you have ample opportunity to prove this, with Venus moving through your Sun sign. You're attractive and can rely on some of your past contacts to make your way into a wider social circle.

On the 9th, meetings with younger people can be more than exhilarating. You'll feel younger and more zestful and there are certainly opportunities that extend beyond your immediate social needs. Collaborative ventures will open doors professionally for you as well.

Too many late nights could cause you to feel run down between the 10th and the 12th. Listen to your body signals, increase your vitamin intake and don't feel obliged to attend every invitation that comes your way, for there are many. Some extra sleep will revitalise those run-down batteries of yours.

Don't gloss over unfinished emotional business on the 14th and 15th. You'll have one last crack at resolving some differences with the person you love. Be quietly assertive without being demanding or overly dominating and you can achieve some great results, which will be long-lasting, indeed.

The telephone call you receive on the 17th or 18th might be rather harrowing. It's imperative for you to keep what you hear private and don't share this information with others. Doing so will be a big mistake and could complicate several relationships for you. Keeping a secret will be the key to peace.

Between the 21st and the 26th, when a lunar eclipse occurs in your zone of marriage and love affairs, important developments are likely in your personal life. Expressing your creativity, serving the one you love and using your personal powers in a wise way will be the secrets to receiving these very same things in return.

Work and money

Between the 5th and the 11th, you'll realise you don't necessarily have to be dishonest to earn money and this can be done through carefully managing your taxation to minimise what you pay the government. You may have been remiss in keeping all your receipts and using some of your day-to-day expenses as a legitimate deduction.

Part of the secret of earning more money between the 15th and the 18th will have to do with the way you present yourself. Polish your shoes, clean your nails and, of course, don't forget to wear a deodorant if you find yourself in hot and uncomfortable situations! A breath freshener wouldn't hurt, either. These are some of the day-to-day things we can sometimes overlook that can have an impact in the success or otherwise of our interactions with others who have the power to make things happen for us.

Personal freedom—breaking free of inhibiting situations—is important to you after the 21st. One door closes and another opens. This is the case with your business relationships on the 26th when the lunar eclipse occurs in your zone of partnerships. Don't hold onto the past and be prepared to let go of something that may have exceeded its 'use by' date.

Destiny dates

Positive: 1, 2, 3, 4, 16, 21, 22, 23, 24, 25, 26, 27, 28
Negative: 12, 14
Mixed: 5, 6, 7, 8, 9, 10, 11, 15, 17, 18

Highlights of the month

July is punctuated by hard work, particularly in your relationships, and this is due to the conjunction of Mars and Saturn in your zone of communications. Over and above this, as mentioned several times in your forecast this year, Saturn will make its presence felt in your domestic sphere, regarding older members of the family and your own inner wellbeing.

Around the 5th it may be important for you to go back over old documents, e-mails that you've misplaced, or text and voice messages that may shed some light on your misunderstanding of a situation. Try to understand that all members of the family may not be quite as adept at remembering facts as you are. The name of the game this month is to try as much as possible to avoid confrontation to make life more peaceful on the home front.

Cancer is known for its ability to help and heal, to show compassion and uplift those who need assistance. If there is someone in your family or a close friend or neighbour you care about, they may be sick or needing some spiritual or psychological guidance. You'll probably find yourself spending large slabs of time advising them and helping them get through the dark night of their soul.

With the solar eclipse occurring in your Sun sign on the 11th, new revelations about your own past and your family members will seem almost like a fiction novel or movie. They do say that 'truth is often stranger than fiction'.

You're extremely idealistic about your love affairs this month, which is due to the close proximity of the Moon with Neptune. Waiting on good news from someone for whom you have affection is very likely during July and, around the 17th or 18th, the anticipation could alter the complexion of your life dramatically, for the better. Dare to dream.

A turn of events in your professional life around the 23rd is likely to make you feel nervous about your future prospects. Don't listen to rumours on the grapevine. Downsizing in your company or your place of work could set off alarm bells, but don't be premature. Look at this as a way of providence granting you the variety you are looking for in your career. It will probably be much more fun than you first imagined once you receive the news of some big change. You must go with the flow.

Between the 28th and 30th don't allow others to force you into a corner, especially if a commitment is required. Work and construction on the home front, dealing with tradespeople or others who may be interested only in the quick buck, could present a problem to you if you are impulsive and less than attentive to the detail of the transaction.

Romance and friendship

Tension is mounting this month, so how will you diffuse the vitalising energy of Mars and Saturn, the Sun and Pluto? Depending how you handle this will determine the outcome of some important relationships.

On the 1st, 3rd and 8th, your personal ethics will be the main component of your discussions. How you've lived and behaved will be mirrored back to you when you make your demands on someone else. Try to be gracious in accepting criticism as a constructive thing. If you fight back and overreact, such resistance will only cause you pain.

There's a solar eclipse on the 11th and this occurs in your Sun sign. This is actually an important spiritual phenomenon that reveals a certain hidden aspect of your personality. Be brave and mature enough to accept that any difficulties you're undergoing in your romantic life are at least in part your own doing. Own your decisions. Take responsibility for them. This will be the lesson that the eclipse teaches you during this cycle.

Between the 14th and the 18th, you'll be seeing love through rose-coloured glasses. Someone you meet will appear like a god to you. Try to remember that everyone has their human frailties and without doubt this person will be no exception to the rule.

You may be greatly disappointed to find that they do indeed have some faults, but you mustn't let this detract from the positive aspects of the friendship. You'll overcome your feelings of regret by the 25th and can resume the relationship on a better footing.

Travel is strongly indicated between the 27th and the 30th. Mercury and the Moon simultaneously moving through your travel zones are all excellent omens indicating cultural exchanges and fun times away from home.

Work and money

Don't go over the top this month in your work. You'll find yourself enlivened by the solar return; that is, the Sun re-entering your Sun sign of Cancer with Mercury. Coupled with this, Jupiter and Uranus strongly bombard your career and self-image.

You'll be pushing hard to meet your deadlines but may at the same time overlook some of the subtleties of what needs to be done. Cutting corners between the 1st and the 4th may be a big mistake. This could result in the wrath of your superiors.

Stay away from work to meet deadlines on the 8th if you need to. Distractions will be harrowing and you're best to do things at your own pace in the comfort and noise-free environment of your own domestic sphere.

A lucky break is likely between the 9th and 13th, especially if you've been waiting on a pay rise. There may have been delays or some complications in this occurring but now you can move ahead with ease.

You'll appreciate a co-worker's kindness on the 31st when they give you a hand with some chore on the work front. Your faith in human nature is restored as a result.

Destiny dates

Positive: 9, 10, 11, 12, 13, 25, 27, 31

Negative: 2, 4, 14, 15, 16, 23

Mixed: 1, 3, 5, 8, 17, 18, 28, 29, 30

Highlights of the month

Being stifled by others is not always a bad thing, especially if they have your best interests at heart. Try not to lock horns with those who are attempting to show you a new or better way of doing things. It will ultimately work in your favour and give you additional skills with which you can further your career.

Between the 1st and the 4th, put on your best listening ears so you can hear what is being said and genuinely try to implement the advice offered to you. Do your best to attempt to move things in the direction that is being suggested. By blocking others you will only find yourself creating a more troublesome period ahead. This could be a test of strength and a battle of wills between you and an employer, but it needn't be.

Creative instincts are triggered due to the favourable influence of Venus between the 7th and the 14th. This is a time to make peace in your family and to smooth over any of the difficulties that once challenged you. Art, craft and recreational activities that bring together your creativity, and the social affairs of your family blend well throughout the month of August.

Venus also represents your ability to love in the truest sense of the word. As it moves into its opposition aspect to the planet Uranus this month, you may be more attracted to the excitement and novelty of 'love' rather than the truer deeper, meaning of it, which involves self-sacrifice, loyalty and genuine affection. For some of you, tasteless affairs may be a form of payback if you're currently in a relationship that is not affording you the satisfaction you would like it to. Be careful you don't do something you'll regret.

If you've thought of making a house move, changing the location where you live, or generally beautifying your surroundings, this is a good time to do so because you have the perfect balance of constructive energy and creativity to make that happen. It's not a bad idea to investigate what's on offer; but again, don't rush headlong into it. Mercury, the planet of communication and contracts, will do its retrograde dance thereby creating uncertainty and even obstacles to achieving your desires. Be patient and rest assured that things happen in their own good time.

On the 28th Jupiter re-enters your powerful career sector, bringing you the resources and opportunities to make appropriate changes in both your personal and professional lives.

Romance and friendship

A dilemma on the home front needs immediate attention between the 7th and the 10th. The combined influence of Saturn and Mars creates a particularly uncomfortable atmosphere. You may not want to be in the company of your family but need to address several issues with them. The space and the location of your home may also be part of the problem that confronts you during this particular cycle.

On the 11th, don't be afraid to communicate your feelings because bottling up that energy will only make it later explode.

The Moon enters your fourth zone of domestic affairs around the 12th and you'll find a greater degree of balance at this time. Things will smooth over when Venus moves into the same sector on the 13th. These two days are highly pivotal to your happiness.

You mustn't accept violence under any circumstances. You may have to deal with such issues between the 5th and 17th, either within your own immediate family circle or involving a friend. Great concern for the welfare of someone you love may cause you to call the authorities or others that can take the appropriate measures to put an end to a painful experience.

If you've taken on the job of renovating your home, you may be in for some surprises between the 20th and the 23rd, when work either grinds to a halt or those you have hired decide to change the terms of agreement.

A temporary move away from your residence is likely or someone may come to stay with you. In any case, this causes some constraints on your natural day-to-day pattern of living and you'll have to use great levels of patience to adjust yourself to these circumstances.

Work and money

Around the 5th, several years of self-examination may culminate in a profound need to move from where you've been. You've learned many lessons and now feel an increasing confidence that you can and must make the break. You can start to build a new future for yourself.

You'll have an appreciation for the past between the 6th and the 10th and will want to make your professional working situation more pleasant and comfortable. Ask for an office makeover if you can't change your location immediately. For example, alter the office furniture by studying the outcomes of *feng shui*, which is the art of correctly placing objects to improve the effects of their electromagnetic energies. This will have a marked impact for the better on your mind and work productivity.

By the 27th, your proposal for changes and a radically different approach to the way in which things are done will be accepted, which will be the start of some new promotional opportunities.

The gathering of information and filing and managing it is also important, especially around the 29th. Updating computers and using modern technology will be related to some big changes taking place in your work.

Destiny dates

Positive: 5, 6, 12, 13, 14, 28, 29
Negative: 15, 16, 17, 20, 21, 22, 23
Mixed: 1, 2, 3, 4, 7, 8, 9, 10, 11

SEPTEMBER

Highlights of the month

You may realise around the 5th that the way you are relating to someone is not exactly warm and loving, but you might not be able to help it. Maybe you are holding onto the past or some transgression against you by them. Forgiveness seems to be one of the main key words for you at this time and, after the 8th when Venus enters your zone of love affairs, you'll find that romance and affection will resume to a normal level.

Single Cancerians can expect a thoroughly lively time romantically and sexually. Who is tugging at your heartstrings? Whomever it is, you'll be feeling lightness in your step and possibly a tingling all over. Avail yourself of the time to develop this feeling and enjoy the benefits that Venus brings.

Parents of kids who have been unruly and diso-bedient will be pleased to see a settling effect by this planet on their personalities. Take the oppor-tunity to spend more quality time with them and create a space in which you can talk about your feelings to develop better relations in the future. If you're dissatisfied with the company that some of your children are keeping, it's best to talk about this when the mood is light and amiable rather than when you've had head-on confrontations.

Mercury moves direct on the 13th of September, so this is a good time to set things straight with others; but make sure you haven't misunderstood their intentions, or you'll get it all wrong. Listening is the active word between the 15th and the 18th.

You have a blatant disregard for the advice that others offer you financially after the 19th, and this could result in a loss of money and possibly even a lowering of your self-esteem and social standing. You have the desire to spend money and also speculate in areas of which you have no knowledge. Mars moving through your fifth zone of speculation and investment indicates a certain level of impulsiveness. Don't let greed rule the day. Having said that, Mars is your luckiest planet and it is likely you will attain something financially beneficial at this time. Just don't let your rash behaviour limit the benefits that could be yours.

Between the 23rd and 30th you may find yourself dissatisfied with your self-image. Are you putting on a few extra kilos? The practical way around this is to keep a 'diet diary' to make notes on your food intake and also your mood swings. It is not enough to lose kilos; you need to work on stabilising your mental and emotional states, too, so that your life will become happier and more pleasant. An exercise regime could now be a good idea.

Romance and friendship

Being reliable and responsible are activities that may not be easy to juggle between the 1st and the 4th. You'll probably feel the pressure of having to do and say things that are not in keeping with how your inner self feels. You may also find yourself torn between two lovers or two friends and have to resort to some form of subtle deception to keep both parties in cahoots.

You continue to seek deep emotional relationships and between the 5th and the 8th may find yourself in a heart-to-heart discussion with a friend or loved one. These discussions will afford you some emotional thrills. For some reason you'll experience greater intensity emotionally and won't be afraid to express how you feel to that person.

You're very passionate this month and this is due to the fact that Mars is moving away from Saturn and in close proximity of Venus. Containing these passions may be difficult for you, particularly between the 11th and the 15th when the Moon moves through your romance sectors in a most powerful way.

A tug of war between duty and emotions will still be a problem for you throughout September, and this will be particularly felt around the 23rd. You could feel restricted and want to break free of these constraints. This requires inventiveness, originality and courage, too.

Between the 28th and 30th, someone may take a swipe at your reputation and there could be little you can do about it. Yet again this may be born out of jealousy or some envy and you're probably aware of who it is. Don't try to meet them head-on as this will only exacerbate the situation.

Work and money

It's not a bad idea to try to improve on some of your professional relationships that have been superficial to date. Between the 5th and the 8th, take time to get to know the people you work with. You'll find yourself suddenly insightful about who they are, what they stand for, and how you and they can actually work more closely to the benefit of all involved.

You'll be the recipient of a rave review or possibly even a reward for your hard work and efforts between the 11th and the 15th. However, the downside is that sometimes a pat on the back may be a disguise for an even greater demand around the corner. You must be aware of this and prepared to brace yourself for some additional responsibility shortly coming your way.

You may be annoyed between the 23rd and the 26th when discussions bog down in the purely theoretical. You'll want a more practical approach to things but may have to deal with others who live in their minds rather than in the real world you inhabit. You'll have no say in how this transpires, so it's best just to go on your merry way and continue working the way you normally do.

Destiny dates

Positive: 6, 7, 8

Negative: 1, 2, 3, 4, 19, 23, 24, 25, 26, 27, 28, 29, 30

Mixed: 5, 11, 12, 13, 15, 16, 17, 18

Highlights of the month

You are extremely passionate in the month of October, as shown by the Venus–Mars combination and the Moon–Pluto opposition. These are powerful forces emotionally and you need to have a clear-cut way of dealing with these primal forces within you. Involving yourself in sport or with a creative art are the easiest ways to redirect these intense feelings.

Between the 1st and 5th your personal responsibilities may require you to give attention elsewhere and this will frustrate you and your partner. Make sure you balance your diary and give enough time to those you love. This will also satisfy your sexual urges. You mustn't turn away from these issues because they are natural and essential aspects of your nature.

If you've been paying too much attention to giving rather than receiving, I suggest you try the latter as a contrast. Balance is always the best policy.

If you need to give impromptu speeches or lectures this month, or attend an important meeting or interview, it's a good idea to have something prepared or at least in the back of your mind for the occasion. You may be a person who doesn't particularly like being the centre of attention, but occasionally it's unavoidable and this could be one of those times. You'll have to be clear-headed, especially around the 12th, so sharpen your thoughts and ideas to avoid going over the whole thing repeatedly.

Leading up to the 20th your educational pursuits will play a dominant part in your life. Reading, studying scripts and other documentation will be most appealing to you. You may rediscover an interest that has lain dormant for many years. This could be part of your genetic history or your karmic make-up, and stumbling upon it may reignite your excitement for life. Finding purpose and true meaning is difficult and, once it happens, there is no point of return.

You'll develop a new relationship with someone at this time that may be based wholly and solely on your intellectual connection. Initially there may be an intense psychological drama that plays out, but this is only because you'll be assessing each other and trying to gain a greater understanding of your philosophies and whether or not you are compatible.

For those of you working in an environment that requires manual exertion, please be careful in the last days of the month between the 28th and 30th. Overexertion can lead to strain and injury.

Romance and friendship

If you're feeling somewhat obscure on the 2nd, you may need to take the initiative and make yourself better known. There's no use complaining about being a wallflower if you're not making an effort to put your best self forward. Get out there, put on your best show, and you'll be surprised at the response you'll get.

You'll feel rebellious, even with your peers, when it comes to your choice of lovers this month. With Mars and Venus powerfully activating your romance sector, the period of the 8th till the 13th is a spicy time, indeed. Your passions heat up and your choice of partners may not at all be in keeping with your past history.

The 10th, 14th, 15th and 18th are important dates to reappraise your physical health. Of primary concern is your cardiovascular system. If you haven't been expressing your feelings openly enough, this could have a marked influence on your physical organs. This is a two-pronged attack—physical and spiritual.

And, speaking of health, the health of an older male or an employer may be spotlighted between the 20th and the 25th. Your sense of responsibility will weigh heavily upon your responses to this person and you'll help out by giving them a hand.

On the 26th, you may overlook an important event only to find out at the last minute that you're ill-prepared to attend the function or party. Make sure your social diary is in order and, more importantly, check it each day.

The Sun conjoining Venus on the 29th is again important for your love affairs. You may have your foot on both the brake and the accelerator at the same time when it comes to some relationship. Either go full steam ahead, or break it off completely.

Work and money

You must strike while the iron is hot on the 2nd. An opportunity like the one appearing now is so few and far between that, if you miss it, you'll kick yourself. A chance to attend a social meeting, a blind date or romantic soiree may not necessarily be taken up by you, even if you feel confident you'll be successful. Perhaps you should rethink staying home?

Performing your work or service will come easily to you around the 6th. You have a lot of energy combined with compassion to contribute to something without any expectation of return. Look at this as an educational exercise that will further upgrade your abilities.

On the 10th, you must keep a close watch on your money or you may just forget what you've done with it. Make sure you collect your receipts.

Between the 11th and the 15th is also a time when you're likely to misplace valuables, including cash. Keep your mind on the moment because it's likely you're a little distracted and this is the cause of your absent-mindedness.

Your boss's wild and outrageous expectations of you may leave you speechless around the 22nd. You'll need time to adjust to their expectations, but may not quite know how to respond at first. Unrealistic demands need to be dealt with by either an extraordinary effort or a steadfast refusal on your part.

Destiny dates

Positive: 2, 6, 12

Negative: 1, 2, 3, 4, 5, 13, 21, 22, 23, 24, 25, 26, 28, 30

Mixed: 10, 14, 15, 18, 20, 29

Highlights of the month

Between the 1st and 7th you may be 'borrowing from Peter to pay Paul'. Your indiscretions may catch up with you and bills could be mounting. Don't lose your cool. You need to be systematic and prioritise which bills need paying first. Many utility companies or banks, for example, are quite willing to discuss and renegotiate the terms of your repayment.

All is not lost so stop making the worst out of a situation that can definitely be improved. Of course, greater responsibility will have to be taken by you in the future to ensure that this doesn't happen again. Creating a budget for yourself and sticking to it will be a key factor in not making the same mistakes.

Expect some fun visitors on the home scene with family members or friends returning from foreign vacations. Between the 8th and 12th, someone coming to stay with you for a while could change the family dynamics. Venus usually brings with it gaiety and social satisfaction so there should be dinners, parties and other pleasant social interactions centred around your home.

Purchasing a car at this time might be difficult but necessary. As already mentioned, the 'debt crisis' will mean you have to tread warily before committing yourself to such a large expenditure. Balance all the pros and cons before making a decision.

Jupiter and Venus together bring you ample good fortune after the 18th. You should purchase your raffle tickets, enter draws at work and even put a dollar or two in the poker machines. But there is no need to overdo it because you are likely to win something during this period.

Being the recipient of some good fortune or a gift will make you more appreciative of what you have rather than what you don't have. You will want to extend yourself by sharing what you have with others and this can give you a sense of fulfilment.

Around the 19th, trying to look flash, savvy and alluring could be your undoing. Whether you are male or female, try to dress for the occasion, be on your best behaviour, and don't drink too much. Manage your self-image and even consider something we often overlook, which is the breath freshener, before going out. Make sure your attire and your personal hygiene is meticulous during this time.

The closing period of the year is excellent for dedicating more time to your relationships so that you can get more out of them. Although work matters will be pressing up to the 22nd, there are moments when you should put aside your own self-interests and invest some time in the ones you love. If previously you have had periods of sexual inhibition or low desire, this can be the perfect opportunity for you to rekindle those feelings of love.

Similarly, if you have had some upsets with your health and been unable to detect exactly what is wrong with you, there is a danger you may resort to pharmaceutical means to solve this problem. However, such a solution could only make matters worse and create a chain effect of further disease and physical imbalance. A suggestion is to take an interest in alternative forms of therapy such as acupuncture, naturopathy, Reiki and meditation. These are worth trying before pumping your body full of artificial chemicals.

Romance and friendship

Apply psychological skill to the relationships you encounter between the 3rd and the 5th, but don't get carried away. Your eager inquisitiveness to get to the root of a person's character and your own self-awareness may pull you away from the reality of the situation.

You may want to overindulge your desires this month, which could be obvious between the 7th and the 11th. Self-restraint will still allow you to have sufficient fun without the after-effects of too much food, sex or alcohol. The interest may be there but you're wiser for resisting the temptation to go over the edge. Apart from that, your wallet probably can't afford it, anyway!

Some good karma comes your way as a result of extending yourself to those in need between the 18th and the 21st. Be gracious enough to accept what's on offer because people get a thrill from giving. If you think you're being polite in turning down a gift or a gesture of gratitude, you may actually be hurting the other person's feelings.

Have that deep and meaningful talk on the 28th if you need to. It's good to get important correspondence out of the way and, all else being equal, you might also just want to take time out, go to the cinema, shut off and enjoy losing yourself in a good thriller or romantic play. Do it with a friend because this will be a perfect blend of creativity and socialising.

A very powerful and alluring one-night stand may be likely on the 30th. You'll be radiating an extra dose of love at this time but your intense sexuality may also have the reverse effect if you come on too strongly.

Work and money

Fire away if you must on the 1st, but make sure the ammunition you're using is not going to damage people in your path. Your plans may need to be adjusted to avoid confrontations with others, especially around the 3rd. Keep your plans moderate until you understand where those around you fit into the scheme of what you intend to do.

Add some extra space into your schedule on the 6th. Figuratively and literally, you may overstep the mark and trip and fall if you're not clear on where you're going around this time. A little extra thought will help prevent missed appointments and also mishaps.

Use those sudden flashes of insight that you have to help you achieve greater success between the 9th and the 16th. You'll be over the humdrum solutions and quite comfortable thinking and working outside the square. Trust your instincts, even if at first others oppose you.

You'll be worried if the phone stops ringing for a while between the 19th and the 26th. Use this to do some effective planning rather than reacting and chasing customers or clients. It will be a quiet time in general.

Destiny dates

Positive: 12, 13, 14, 15, 16, 18, 28, 30

Negative: 1, 2, 7

Mixed 3, 4, 5, 6, 8, 9, 10, 11, 19, 20, 21, 22, 23, 24, 25, 26

Highlights of the month

In the final month of 2010 you have the desire to stand out and be recognised as unique, but this may be difficult if you are dealing with people who are stuck in their old ways. On the 1st, when Mercury enters your zone of public relations, you'll be more likely than usual to want to discuss these differences and find some resolution.

With Christmas around the corner you could be quite distracted between the 2nd and the 7th and you won't be able to keep your mind on the job at hand. This inattentiveness might not only have something to do with the excitement in the air generated by gift giving or office parties, etc., but a lingering dissatisfaction with the work you are performing. It may be a little late in the year to effect any real changes, but it's always a good policy to investigate what's on offer and analyse how things can be better in the coming year. This is a time of re-appraisal.

Mars enters the marital zone of your horoscope and brings with it some difficulties, arguments and irritability. You and your partner need to give each other space and it is probably better not to work too closely with the ones you love at this time. If you run an independent business involving family members, why not schedule in some independent tasks so that you are not in each other's way? This will ensure the lead up to Christmas is much smoother, thereby avoiding the Christmas dinner explosions that are found in many families across the world.

The energies for Cancer leading up to Christmas are indeed very powerful and the most notable astrological influence would have to be the lunar eclipse on the 21st in the sign of Gemini. A huge amount of power can be released under the eclipse and for you it will herald an important spiritual lesson in letting go of the past, living in the present and letting bygones be bygones. This is a healing time and Christmas 2010 should be a season of forgiveness, not so much one of gift giving. The greatest gift you may be able to give someone is that of forgiveness and a handshake. The closing theme of 2010 must surely be that of restoration and regeneration.

Romance and friendship

You'll be curious about someone between the 1st and the 3rd but may not know enough about them to feel confident enough to 'give them the green light', emotionally speaking. You could do some fact finding on the sly; but, of course, your honesty and integrity should stand as the key features of your interaction with this person. What you come to learn about them may not be all that rosy, but you'll still be enamoured enough to develop a bit more of a relationship with them.

Things can heat up in your friendships around the 9th, but you may suddenly do an about-face on the 10th when Mercury goes retrograde. You'll find some apparent contradictions in what others say and this will bother you. However, before jumping to conclusions, measure what is being said against the background and context in which you find yourself. The situation could make more sense afterwards.

You may be saying yes to far too many people on the 16th. Only shoulder what you can comfortably carry; but by the same token, don't put yourself in the situation where you miss valuable social opportunities.

Leading up to Christmas, weeding out those who are unacceptable friends will be important, especially between the 21st and the 23rd. You will finally have to let go of people who have done little to enhance your life. You can thank the lunar eclipse for this.

As the year winds down, and in particular between the 24th and the 29th, an old chapter of your life will close and a new one will open. Some people will come, and some will go, but it will be obvious that the wisdom you've gained will hold you in good stead in the coming years.

You'll be entering a new and intense phase romantically and socially, and the forward motion of Mercury on the 30th gives you even greater confidence that the decisions you've come to make, as hard as some of them might have been, are certainly the best for you and others concerned.

Work and money

The rules of the game are changing in your professional arena. On the 4th, this may be highlighted by the fact that the directives you're given will be completely turned around, much to your amazement. There's more to the job than you had first expected, and others may be purposely keeping you in the dark.

You need to enforce some new diplomatic rules of your own between the 11th and the 16th. With work getting more hectic leading up to Christmas, you mustn't allow yourself to be placed in an embarrassing situation by not being up to scratch with your behaviour or your work ethic.

Between the 22nd and the 24th, you have the opportunity to speak your mind and identify clearly the problems that are holding you back. You'll gain some Brownie points by calling the situation as you see it.

Mercury's forward movement on the 30th and 31st is an excellent omen, indicating clarity in your contracts and an assurance from others that you have the continuing support you need to forge an even more successful future in the coming twelve months. Congratulations on a job well done throughout 2010, Cancer.

Destiny dates

Positive: 1, 9, 24, 25, 26, 27, 28, 29, 30, 31
Negative: 5, 6, 7, 10, 11, 12, 13, 14, 15, 16
Mixed: 2, 3, 4, 21, 22, 23

2010:
Astronumerology

*The more business a man has to do, the more he is able
to accomplish, for he learns to economize his time.*

—Sir Matthew Hale

The power behind your name

By adding the numbers of your name you can see
which planet is ruling you. Each of the letters of
the alphabet is assigned a number, which is listed
below. These numbers are ruled by the planets.
This is according to the ancient Chaldean system of
numerology and is very different to the Pythagorean
system to which many refer.

Each number is assigned a planet:

AIQJY	=	1	**Sun**
BKR	=	2	**Moon**
CGLS	=	3	**Jupiter**
DMT	=	4	**Uranus**
EHNX	=	5	**Mercury**
UVW	=	6	**Venus**
OZ	=	7	**Neptune**
FP	=	8	**Saturn**
—	=	9	**Mars**

Notice that the number 9 is not aligned with a letter
because it is considered special. Once the numbers
have been added you will see that a single planet
rules your name and personal affairs. Many famous

actors, writers and musicians change their names to attract the energy of a luckier planet. You can experiment with the list and try new names or add the letters of your second name to see how that vibration suits you. It's a lot of fun!

Here is an example of how to find out the power of your name. If your name is John Smith, calculate the ruling planet by assigning each letter to a number in the table like this:

J O H N S M I T H
1 7 5 5 3 4 1 4 5

Now add the numbers like this:
$1 + 7 + 5 + 5 + 3 + 4 + 1 + 4 + 5 = 35$
Then add $3 + 5 = 8$

The ruling number of John Smith's name is 8, which is ruled by Saturn. Now study the name-number table to reveal the power of your name. The numbers 3 and 5 will also play a secondary role in John's character and destiny, so in this case you would also study the effects of Jupiter and Mercury.

SUSAN   TOPLEY
36315   478351 = 46 = 10 = 1?

SUSAN ANNE   TOPLEY
36315 1555   478351 = 62 = 8

$1 + 4 + 7 + 2 + 0 + 1 + 0 = 15 = 6$
or $8 + 2 + 0 + 1 + 0 = 11 = 2$

Name-number table

Your name number	Ruling planet	Your name characteristics
1	**Sun**	Magnetic individual. Great energy and life force. Physically dynamic and sociable. Attracts good friends and individuals in powerful positions. Good government connections. Intelligent, impressive, flashy and victorious. A loyal number for relationships.
2	**Moon**	Soft, emotional nature. Changeable moods but psychic, intuitive senses. Imaginative nature and empathetic expression of feelings. Loves family, mother and home life. Night owl who probably needs more sleep. Success with the public and/or women.
3	**Jupiter**	Outgoing, optimistic number with lucky overtones. Attracts opportunities without trying. Good sense of timing. Religious or spiritual aspirations.

Your name number	Ruling planet	Your name characteristics
		Can investigate the meaning of life. Loves to travel and explore the world and people.
4	Uranus	Explosive character with many unusual aspects. Likes the untried and novel. Forward thinking, with many extra-ordinary friends. Gets fed up easily so needs plenty of invigorating experiences. Pioneering, technological and imaginative. Wilful and stubborn when wants to be. Unexpected events in life may be positive or negative.
5	Mercury	Quick-thinking mind with great powers of speech. Extremely vigorous life; always on the go and lives on nervous energy. Youthful attitude and never grows old. Looks younger than actual age. Young friends and humorous disposition. Loves reading and writing.
6	Venus	Delightful personality. Graceful and attractive character who cherishes friends

Your name number	Ruling planet	Your name characteristics
		and social life. Musical or artistic interests. Good for money making as well as abundant love affairs. Career in the public eye is possible. Loves family but is often overly concerned by friends.
7	Neptune	Intuitive, spiritual and self-sacrificing nature. Easily misled by those who need help. Loves to dream of life's possibilities. Has curative powers. Dreams are revealing and prophetic. Loves the water and will have many journeys in life. Spiritual aspirations dominate worldly desires.
8	Saturn	Hard-working, focused individual with slow but certain success. Incredible concentration and self-sacrifice for a goal.
		Money orientated but generous when trust is gained. Professional but may be a hard taskmaster. Demands

		highest standards and needs to learn to enjoy life a little more.
9	**Mars**	Fantastic physical drive and ambition. Sports and outdoor activities are keys to wellbeing. Confrontational. Likes to work and play just as hard. Caring and protective of family, friends and territory. Individual tastes in life but is also self-absorbed. Needs to listen to others' advice to gain greater success.

Your 2010 planetary ruler

Astrology and numerology are very intimately connected. As already shown, each planet rules over a number between 1 and 9. Both your name *and* your birth date are ruled by planetary energies.

Add the numbers of your birth date and the year in question to find out which planet will control the coming year for you.

For example, if you were born on the 12th of November, add the numerals 1 and 2 (12, your day of birth) and 1 and 1 (11, your month of birth) to the year in question, in this case 2010 (the current year), like this:

$1 + 2 + 1 + 1 + 2 + 0 + 1 + 0 = 8$

The planet ruling your individual karma for 2010 will be Saturn because this planet rules the number 8.

You can even take your ruling name-number as shown earlier and add it to the year in question to throw more light on your coming personal affairs, like this:

John Smith = 8

Year coming = 2010

$8 + 2 + 0 + 1 + 0 = 11$

$1 + 1 = 2$

Therefore, 2 is the ruling number of the combined name and date vibrations. Study the Moon's number 2 influence for 2010.

Outlines of the year number ruled by each planet are given below. Enjoy!

1 is the year of the Sun

Overview

The Sun is the brightest object in the heavens and rules number 1 and the sign of Leo. Because of this the coming year will bring you great success and popularity.

You'll be full of life and radiant vibrations and are more than ready to tackle your new nine-year cycle, which begins now. Any new projects you commence are likely to be successful.

Your health and vitality will be very strong and your stamina at its peak. Even if you happen to have the odd problem with your health, your recuperative power will be strong.

You have tremendous magnetism this year so social popularity won't be a problem for you. I see many new friends and lovers coming into your life. Expect loads of invitations to parties and fun-filled outings. Just don't take your health for granted as you're likely to burn the candle at both ends.

With success coming your way, don't let it go to your head. You must maintain humility, which will make you even more popular in the coming year.

Love and pleasure

This is an important cycle for renewing your love and connections with your family, particularly if you have children. The Sun is connected with the sign of Leo and therefore brings an increase in musical and theatrical activities. Entertainment and other creative hobbies will be high on your agenda and bring you a great sense of satisfaction.

Work

You won't have to make too much of an effort to be successful this year because the brightness of the Sun will draw opportunities to you. Changes in work are likely and, if you have been concerned that opportunities are few and far between, 2010 will be different. You can expect some sort of promotion or an increase in income because your employers will take special note of your skills and service orientation.

Improving your luck

Leo is the ruler of number 1 and, therefore, if you're born under this star sign, 2010 will be particularly lucky. For others, July and August, the months of Leo, will bring good fortune. The 1st, 8th, 15th and 22nd hours of Sundays especially will give you a unique sort of luck in any sort of competition or activities generally. Keep your eye out for those born under Leo as they may be able to contribute something to your life and may even have a karmic connection to you. This is a particularly important year for your destiny.

Your lucky numbers in this coming cycle are 1, 10, 19 and 28.

2 is the year of the Moon
Overview

There's nothing more soothing than the cool light of the full Moon on a clear night. The Moon is emotional and receptive and controls your destiny in 2010. If you're able to use the positive energies of the Moon, it will be a great year in which you can realign and improve your relationships, particularly with family members.

Making a commitment to becoming a better person and bringing your emotions under control will also dominate your thinking. Try not to let your emotions get the better of you throughout the coming year because you may be drawn into the changeable nature of these lunar vibrations as well. If you fail to keep control of your emotional life you'll later regret some of your actions. You must blend careful thinking with feeling to arrive at the best results. Your luck throughout 2010 will certainly be determined by the state of your mind.

Because the Moon and the sign of Cancer rule the number 2 there is a certain amount of change to be expected this year. Keep your feelings steady and don't let your heart rule your head.

Love and pleasure

Your primary concern in 2010 will be your home and family life. You'll be finally keen to take on those renovations, or work on your garden. You may even think of buying a new home. You can at last carry out some of those plans and make your dreams come true. If you find yourself a little more temperamental than usual, do some extra meditation and spend time alone until you sort this out. You mustn't withhold your feelings from your partner as this will only create frustration.

Work

During 2010 your focus will be primarily on feelings and family; however, this doesn't mean you can't make great strides in your work as well. The Moon rules the general public and what you might find is that special opportunities and connections with the world at large present themselves to you. You could be working with large numbers of people.

If you're looking for a better work opportunity, try to focus your attention on women who can give you a hand. Use your intuition as it will be finely tuned this year. Work and career success depends upon your instincts.

Improving your luck

The sign of Cancer is your ruler this year and because the Moon rules Mondays, both this day of the week and the month of July are extremely lucky for you. The 1st, 8th, 15th and 22nd hours on Mondays will be very powerful. Pay special attention to the new and full Moon days throughout 2010.

The numbers 2, 11 and 29 are lucky for you.

3 is the year of Jupiter

Overview

The year 2010 will be a number 3 year for you and, because of this, Jupiter and Sagittarius will dominate your affairs. This is extremely lucky and shows you'll be motivated to broaden your horizons, gain more money and become extremely popular in your social circles. It looks like 2010 will be a fun-filled year with much excitement.

Jupiter and Sagittarius are generous to a fault and so, likewise, your open-handedness will mark the year. You'll be friendly and helpful to all of those around you.

Pisces is also under the rulership of the number 3 and this brings out your spiritual and compassion-ate nature. You'll become a much better person, reducing your negative karma by increasing your self-awareness and spiritual feelings. You will want to share your luck with those you love.

Love and pleasure

Travel and seeking new adventures will be part and parcel of your romantic life this year. Travelling to distant lands and meeting unusual people will open your heart to fresh possibilities of romance.

You'll try novel and audacious things and will find yourself in a different circle of friends. Compromise will be important in making your existing relationships work. Talk about your feelings. If you are currently in a relationship you'll feel an upswing in your affection for your partner. This is a perfect opportunity to deepen your love for each other and take your relationship to a new level.

If you're not yet attached to someone, there's good news for you. Great opportunities lie in store and a spiritual or karmic connection may be experienced in 2010.

Work

Great fortune can be expected through your working life in the next twelve months. Your friends and work colleagues will want to help you achieve your goals. Even your employers will be amenable to your requests for extra money or a better position within the organisation.

If you want to start a new job or possibly begin an independent line of business, this is a great year to do it. Jupiter looks set to give you plenty of opportunities, success and a superior reputation.

Improving your luck

As long as you can keep a balanced view of things and not overdo anything, your luck will increase dramatically throughout 2010. The important thing is to remain grounded and not be too airy-fairy about your objectives. Be realistic about your talents and capabilities and don't brag about your skills or achievements. This will only invite envy from others.

Moderate your social life as well and don't drink or eat too much as this will slow your reflexes and weaken your chances for success.

You have plenty of spiritual insights this year so you should use them to their maximum. In the 1st, 8th, 15th and 24th hours of Thursdays you should use your intuition to enhance your luck, and the numbers 3, 12, 21 and 30 are also lucky for you. March and December are your lucky months but generally the whole year should go pretty smoothly for you.

4 is the year of Uranus

Overview

The electric and exciting planet of the zodiac, Uranus, and its sign of Aquarius, rule your affairs throughout 2010. Dramatic events will surprise and at the same time unnerve you in your professional and personal life. So be prepared!

You'll be able to achieve many things this year and your dreams are likely to come true, but you mustn't be distracted or scattered with your energies. You'll be breaking through your own self-limitations and this will present challenges from your family and friends. You'll want to be independent and develop your spiritual powers and nothing will stop you.

Try to maintain discipline and an orderly lifestyle so you can make the most of these special energies this year. If unexpected things do happen, it's not a bad idea to have an alternative plan so you don't lose momentum.

Love and pleasure

You want something radical, something different in your relationships this year. It's quite likely that your love life will be feeling a little less than exciting so you'll take some important steps to change that. If your partner is as progressive as you'll be this year, then your relationship is likely to improve and fulfil both of you.

In your social life you will meet some very unusual people, whom you'll feel are especially connected to you spiritually. You may want to ditch everything for the excitement and passion of a completely new relationship, but tread carefully as this may not work out exactly as you expect it to.

Work

Technology, computing and the Internet will play a larger role in your professional life this coming year.

You'll have to move ahead with the times and learn new skills if you want to achieve success.

A hectic schedule is likely, so make sure your diary is with you at all times. Try to be more efficient and don't waste time.

New friends and alliances at work will help you achieve even greater success in the coming period. Becoming a team player will be even more important in gaining satisfaction from your professional endeavours.

Improving your luck

Moving too quickly and impulsively will cause you problems on all fronts, so be a little more patient and think your decisions through more carefully. Social, romantic and professional opportunities will come to you but take a little time to investigate the ramifications of your actions.

The 1st, 8th, 15th and 20th hours of any Saturday are lucky, but love and luck are likely to cross your path when you least expect it. The numbers 4, 13, 22 and 31 are also lucky for you this year.

5 is the year of Mercury

Overview

The supreme planet of communication, Mercury, is your ruling planet throughout 2010. The number 5, which is connected to Mercury, will confer upon you success through your intellectual abilities.

Any form of writing or speaking will be improved and this will be, to a large extent, underpinning your success. Your imagination will be stimulated by this planet, with many incredible new and exciting ideas coming to mind.

Mercury and the number 5 are considered somewhat indecisive. Be firm in your attitude and don't let too many ideas or opportunities distract and confuse you. By all means get as much information as you can to help you make the right decisions.

I see you involved with money proposals, job applications, even contracts that need to be signed, so remain as clear-headed as possible.

Your business skills and clear and concise communication will be at the heart of your life in 2010.

Love and pleasure

Mercury, which rules the signs of Gemini and Virgo, will make your love life a little difficult due to its changeable nature. On the one hand you'll feel passionate and loving to your partner, yet on the other you will feel like giving it all up for the excitement of a new affair. Maintain the middle ground.

Also, try not to be too critical with your friends and family members. The influence of Virgo makes you prone to expecting much more from others than they're capable of giving. Control your sharp tongue and don't hurt people's feelings. Encouraging others is the better path, leading to greater emotional satisfaction.

Work

Speed will dominate your professional life in 2010. You'll be flitting from one subject to another and taking on far more than you can handle. You'll need to make some serious changes in your routine to handle the avalanche of work that will come your way. You'll also be travelling with your work, but not necessarily overseas.

If you're in a job you enjoy then this year will give you additional successes. If not, it may be time to move on.

Improving your luck

Communication is the key to attaining your desires in the coming twelve months. Keep focused on one idea rather than scattering your energies in all directions and your success will be speedier.

By looking after your health, sleeping well and exercising regularly, you'll build up your resilience and mental strength.

The 1st, 8th, 15th and 20th hours of Wednesday are lucky so it's best to schedule your meetings and other important social engagements during these times. The lucky numbers for Mercury are 5, 14, 23 and 32.

6 is the year of Venus

Overview

Because you're ruled by 6 this year, love is in the air! Venus, Taurus and Libra are well known for their affinity with romance, love, and even marriage. If ever you were going to meet a soulmate and feel comfortable in love, 2010 must surely be your year.

Taurus has a strong connection to money and practical affairs as well, so finances will also improve if you are diligent about work and security issues.

The important thing to keep in mind this year is that sharing love and making that important soul connection should be kept high on your agenda. This will be an enjoyable period in your life.

Love and pleasure

Romance is the key thing for you this year and your current relationships will become more fulfilling if you happen to be attached. For singles, a 6 year heralds an important meeting that eventually leads to marriage.

You'll also be interested in fashion, gifts, jewellery and all sorts of socialising. It's at one of these social engagements that you could meet the love of your life. Remain available!

Venus is one of the planets that has a tendency to overdo things, so be moderate in your eating and drinking. Try generally to maintain a modest lifestyle.

Work

You'll have a clearer insight into finances and your future security during a number 6 year. Whereas previously you may have had additional expenses and extra distractions, your mind will now be more settled and capable of longer-term planning along these lines.

With the extra cash you might see this year, decorating your home or office will give you a special sort of satisfaction.

Social affairs and professional activities will be strongly linked. Any sort of work-related functions may offer you romantic opportunities as well. On the other hand, be careful not to mix up your workplace relationships with romantic ideals. This could complicate some of your professional activities.

Improving your luck

You'll want more money and a life of leisure and ease in 2010. Keep working on your strengths and eliminate your negative personality traits to create greater luck and harmony in your life.

Moderate all your actions and don't focus exclusively on money and material objects. Feed your spiritual needs as well. By balancing your inner and outer sides you'll see that your romantic and professional lives will be enhanced more easily.

The 1st, 8th, 15th and 20th hours on Fridays will be very lucky for you and new opportunities will arise for you at those times. You can use the numbers 6, 15, 24 and 33 to increase luck in your general affairs.

7 is the year of Neptune

Overview

The last and most evolved sign of the zodiac is

Pisces, which is ruled by Neptune. The number 7 is deeply connected with this zodiac sign and governs you in 2010. Your ideals seem to be clearer and more spiritually orientated than ever before. Your desire to evolve and understand your inner self will be a double-edged sword. It depends on how organised you are as to how well you can use these spiritual and abstract concepts in your practical life.

Your past hurts and deep emotional issues will be dealt with and removed for good, if you are serious about becoming a better human being.

Spend a little more time caring for yourself rather than others, as it's likely some of your friends will drain you of energy with their own personal problems. Of course, you mustn't turn a blind eye to the needs of others, but don't ignore your own personal requirements in the process.

Love and pleasure

Meeting people with similar life views and spiritual aspirations will rekindle your faith in relationships. If you do choose to develop a new romance, make sure there is a clear understanding of the responsibilities of one to the other. Don't get swept off your feet by people who have ulterior motives.

Keep your relationships realistic and see that the most idealistic partnerships must eventually come down to Earth. Deal with the practicalities of life.

Work

This is a year of hard work, but one in which you'll

come to understand the deeper significance of your professional ideals. You may discover a whole new aspect to your career, which involves a more compassionate and self-sacrificing side to your personality.

You'll also find that your way of working will change and you'll be more focused and able to get into the spirit of whatever you do. Finding meaningful work is very likely and therefore this could be a year when money, security, creativity and spirituality overlap to bring you a great sense of personal satisfaction.

Tapping into your greater self through meditation and self-study will bring you great benefits throughout 2010.

Improving your luck

Using self-sacrifice along with discrimination will be an unusual method of improving your luck. The laws of karma state that what you give, you receive in greater measure. This is one of the principal themes for you in 2010.

The 1st, 8th, 15th and 20th hours of Tuesdays are your lucky times. The numbers 7, 16, 25 and 34 should be used to increase your lucky energies.

8 is the year of Saturn

Overview

The earthy and practical sign of Capricorn and its ruler Saturn are intimately linked to the number

8, which rules you in 2010. Your discipline and far-sightedness will help you achieve great things in the coming year. With cautious discernment, slowly but surely you will reach your goals.

It may be that due to the influence of the solitary Saturn, your best work and achievement will be behind closed doors away from the limelight. You mustn't fear this as you'll discover many new things about yourself. You'll learn just how strong you really are.

Love and pleasure

Work will overshadow your personal affairs in 2010, but you mustn't let this erode the personal relationships you have. Becoming a workaholic brings great material successes but will also cause you to become too insular and aloof. Your family members won't take too kindly to you working 100-hour weeks.

Responsibility is one of the key words for this number and you will therefore find yourself in a position of authority that leaves very little time for fun. Try to make the time to enjoy the company of friends and family and by all means schedule time off on the weekends as it will give you the peace of mind you're looking for.

Because of your responsible attitude it will be very hard for you not to assume a greater role in your workplace and this indicates longer working hours with the likelihood of a promotion with equally good remuneration.

Work

Money is high on your agenda in 2010. Number 8 is a good money number according to the Chinese and this year is at last likely to bring you the fruits of your hard labour. You are cautious and resourceful in all your dealings and will not waste your hard-earned savings. You will also be very conscious of using your time wisely.

You will be given more responsibilities and you're likely to take them on, if only to prove to yourself that you can handle whatever life dishes up.

Expect a promotion in which you'll play a leading role in your work. Your diligence and hard work will pay off, literally, in a bigger salary and more respect from others.

Improving your luck

Caution is one of the key characteristics of the number 8 and is linked to Capricorn. But being overly cautious could cause you to miss valuable opportunities. If an offer is put to you, try to think outside the square and balance it with your naturally cautious nature.

Be gentle and kind to yourself. By loving yourself, others will naturally love you, too. The 1st, 8th, 15th and 20th hours of Saturdays are exceptionally lucky for you, as are the numbers 1, 8, 17, 26 and 35.

9 is the year of Mars

Overview

You are now entering the final year of a nine-year cycle dominated by the planet Mars and the sign of Aries. You'll be completing many things and are determined to be successful after several years of intense work.

Some of your relationships may now have reached their use-by date and even personal affairs may need to be released. Don't let arguments and disagreements get in the road of friendly resolution in these areas of your life.

Mars is a challenging planet, and this year, although you will be very active and productive, you may find others trying to obstruct the achievement of your goals. As a result you may react strongly to them, thereby creating disharmony in your workplace. Don't be so impulsive or reckless, and generally slow things down. The slower, steadier approach has greater merit this year.

Love and pleasure

If you become too bossy and pushy with friends this year you will just end up pushing them out of your life. It's a year to end certain friendships but by the same token it could be the perfect time to remove conflicts and thereby bolster your love affairs in 2010.

If you're feeling a little irritable and angry with those you love, try getting rid of these negative feelings through some intense, rigorous sports and physical activity. This will definitely relieve tension and improve your personal life.

Work

Because you're healthy and able to work at a more intense pace you'll achieve an incredible amount in the coming year. Overwork could become a problem if you're not careful.

Because the number 9 and Mars are infused with leadership energy, you'll be asked to take the reins of the job and steer your company or group in a certain direction. This will bring with it added responsibility but also a greater sense of purpose for you.

Improving your luck

Because of the hot and restless energy of the number 9, it is important to create more mental peace in your life this year. Lower the temperature, so to speak, and decompress your relationships rather than becoming aggravated. Try to talk with your work partners and loved ones rather than telling them what to do. This will generally pick up your health and your relationships.

The 1st, 8th, 15th and 20th hours of Tuesdays are the luckiest for you this year and, if you're involved in any disputes or need to attend to health issues, these times are also very good to get the best results. Your lucky numbers are 9, 18, 27 and 36.

CANCER

2010:
Your Daily Planner

*You cannot plough a field by turning it over
in your mind*

—Author unknown

According to astrology, the success of any venture or activity is dependent upon the planetary positions at the time you commence that activity. Electional astrology helps you select the most appropriate times for many of your day-to-day endeavours. These dates are applicable to each and every zodiac sign and can be used freely by one and all, even if your star sign doesn't fall under the one mentioned in this book. Please note that the daily planner is a universal system applicable equally to all *twelve* star signs. Anyone and everyone can use this planner irrespective of their birth sign.

Ancient astrologers understood the planetary patterns and how they impacted on each of us. This allowed them to suggest the best possible times to start various important activities. For example, many farmers still use this approach today: they understand the phases of the Moon, and attest to the fact that planting seeds on certain lunar days produces a far better crop than does planting on other days.

In the following section, many facets of daily life are considered. Using the lunar cycle and the combined strength of other planets allows us to work out the best times to do them. This is your personal almanac, which can be used in conjunction with any star sign to help optimise the results.

First, select the activity you are interested in, and then quickly scan the year for the best months to start it. When you have selected the month, you can finetune your timing by finding the best specific dates. You can then be sure that the planetary energies will be in sync with you, offering you the best possible outcome.

Coupled with what you know about your monthly and weekly trends, the daily planner is an effective tool to help you capitalise on opportunities that come your way this year.

Good luck, and may the planets bless you with great success, fortune and happiness in 2010!

Getting started in 2010

How many times have you made a new year's resolution to begin a diet or be a better person in your relationships? And, how many times has it not worked out? Well, part of the reason may be that you started out at the wrong time, because how successful you are is strongly influenced by the position of the Moon and the planets when you begin a particular activity. You will be more successful with the following endeavours if you start them on the days indicated.

Relationships

We all feel more empowered on some days than on others. This is because the planets have some power over us—their movement and their relationships to each other determine the ebb and flow of our energies. And, our levels of self-confidence and sense of romantic magnetism play an important part in the way we behave in relationships.

Your daily planner tells you the ideal dates for meeting new friends, initiating a love affair, spending time with family and loved ones—it even tells you the most appropriate times for sexual encounters.

You'll be surprised at how much more impact you will make in your relationships when you tune yourself in to the planetary energies on these special dates.

Falling in love/restoring love

During these times you could expect favourable energies to meet your soulmate or, if you've had difficulty in a relationship, to approach the one you love to rekindle both your and their emotional responses:

January	18, 20, 23, 24
February	15, 16, 20, 24
March	29
April	16
May	14, 17, 18, 19, 20, 23
June	14, 15, 16, 20, 21
July	12
August	10, 13, 14
September	9, 21, 22
October	8, 18, 19, 20
November	14, 15, 16, 19, 20, 21
December	13, 17, 18

Special times with friends and family

Socialising, partying and having a good time with those whose company you enjoy is highly favourable under the following dates. They are excellent to spend time with family and loved ones in a domestic environment:

January	6, 26, 27
February	12, 13, 14, 15, 16, 20, 24
March	11, 21, 22, 29, 30, 31
April	8
May	15, 16, 17, 18, 19, 20, 23, 24
June	1, 2, 3, 11, 12, 14, 15, 16, 20, 21, 29, 30
July	8, 9, 12, 17, 18, 26, 27
August	5, 6, 9, 10, 13, 14, 22, 23, 24
September	1, 2, 5, 9, 10, 18, 19, 20, 30
October	3, 19, 20, 25, 26, 30, 31
November	3, 4, 14, 15, 16, 22, 26, 27
December	2, 9, 10, 11, 19, 20, 24, 25

Healing or resuming relationships

If you're trying to get back together with the one you love or need a heart-to-heart or deep-and-meaningful discussion with someone, you can try the following dates to do so:

January	12, 13, 14, 15, 21, 22, 23, 24, 25
February	6
March	6, 31
April	2, 7, 8, 12, 16, 19, 23, 24, 25, 26

May	10, 11, 12, 13, 14, 15, 16, 17, 18, 19, 20, 21, 22, 23, 24, 25, 26, 27, 28, 30
June	3, 8, 9, 10, 11, 12, 13, 14, 15, 16, 17, 21, 22, 23, 25, 26, 27, 28, 29, 30
July	1, 2, 3, 4, 5, 10, 11, 12, 13, 15, 16, 17, 18, 19, 20, 21, 22, 23, 28, 29, 30
August	1, 2, 3, 4, 5, 6, 9, 10, 13, 14, 15, 16, 20, 23, 25, 26, 27
September	2, 5, 9, 10, 13, 17, 18, 19, 20
October	1, 2, 3, 6, 12, 13, 14, 15, 20, 22, 23, 24, 25, 26, 27, 28, 29, 30, 31
November	3, 4, 5, 6, 7, 8, 9, 21, 27, 28, 29, 30
December	2, 3, 4, 6, 12, 13, 14, 17, 18, 19, 20, 21, 23, 24, 25

Sexual encounters

Physical and sexual energies are well favoured on the following dates. The energies of the planets enhance your moments of intimacy during these times:

January	1, 6, 7, 21, 22
February	6, 12, 13, 14, 20, 24
March	14, 15, 17, 18, 19, 30, 31
April	23, 24, 25, 26
May	9, 12, 14, 17, 18, 19, 20
June	3, 8, 9, 10, 11, 14, 15, 16, 20, 21, 29, 30
July	8, 9, 10, 11, 12
August	6, 10, 13, 14, 22, 23, 24

September	3, 4, 5, 6, 9, 10, 18, 19, 20, 21, 22, 30
October	1, 2, 3, 7, 8, 18, 19, 20, 23, 24, 28, 29, 30, 31
November	3, 4, 14, 15, 16, 19, 24, 25, 26, 27
December	2, 10, 11, 12, 13, 15, 16, 17, 19, 20, 22, 23, 24, 25

Health and wellbeing

Your aura and life force are susceptible to the movements of the planets—in particular, they respond to the phases of the Moon.

The following dates are the most appropriate times to begin a diet, have cosmetic surgery, or seek medical advice. They also indicate the best times to help others.

Feeling of wellbeing

Your physical as well as your mental alertness should be strong on these following dates. You can plan your activities and expect a good response from others:

January	2, 3, 4, 5, 6, 7, 11, 12, 13, 14, 16, 17, 18, 21, 22, 23, 24, 30, 31
February	1, 2, 7, 8, 15, 16, 17, 18, 19, 20, 21, 22, 23, 24, 25, 26, 27, 28
March	16, 17, 18, 19, 20, 22, 23, 24, 25, 26, 27, 28, 29
April	7, 13, 14, 16, 28
May	2, 11, 14, 25, 26
June	8, 22, 23, 26, 27, 28, 29, 30

July	4, 5, 8, 9, 12, 13, 14, 15, 16, 19, 20, 23, 24, 25
August	5, 6, 9, 10, 11, 12, 13, 15, 16, 20, 21
September	9, 10, 11, 12, 13, 16, 17, 21, 22, 24, 25, 28, 29, 30
October	3, 4, 5, 6, 7, 8, 9, 10, 13, 14, 15, 22
November	4, 5, 6, 10, 11, 19, 20, 21
December	7, 8, 17, 18, 28, 29

Healing and medicine

These times are good for approaching others who have expertise when you need some deeper understanding. They are also favourable for any sort of healing or medication and making appointments with doctors or psychologists. Planning surgery around these dates should bring good results.

Often giving up our time and energy to assist others doesn't necessarily result in the expected outcome. However, by lending a helping hand to a friend on the following dates, the results should be favourable:

January	1, 2, 3, 4, 6, 7, 8, 9, 11, 12, 13, 14, 15, 16, 17, 18, 19, 20, 21, 22, 23, 24, 26, 27, 28, 29, 30, 31
February	1, 5, 6, 9, 11, 12, 13, 14, 15, 16, 19
March	1, 2, 3, 4, 5, 8, 9, 10, 11, 12, 18, 19, 24, 25, 29
April	1, 3, 4, 5, 22, 26
May	4, 5

175

June	1, 2, 3, 9, 10, 17, 18, 22, 23, 24, 25, 29, 30
July	6, 7, 15, 16, 17, 18, 19, 21, 22, 23, 24, 25, 26
August	2, 3, 4, 11, 12, 17, 18, 19, 20, 21, 30, 31
September	6, 7, 8, 10, 11, 12, 13, 14, 15, 16, 17, 18, 26, 27, 28, 29
October	5, 7, 8, 9, 10, 11, 12, 13, 14, 15, 16, 17, 18, 19, 20, 21, 22, 23, 24, 25, 26, 28, 29, 30, 31
November	1, 2, 3, 5, 7, 8, 10, 11, 14, 15, 17, 18, 19, 22, 23
December	4, 5, 7, 8, 9, 10, 12, 13, 14, 16, 23, 24, 25, 26, 28, 29, 30, 31

Money

Money is an important part of life, and involves many decisions—decisions about borrowing, investing, spending. The ideal times for transactions are very much influenced by the planets, and whether your investment or nest egg grows or doesn't grow can often be linked to timing. Making your decisions on the following dates could give you a whole new perspective on your financial future.

Managing wealth and money

To build your nest egg it's a good time to open your bank account or invest money on the following dates:

January	1, 6, 7, 13, 14, 15, 18, 21, 22, 28, 29
February	3, 4, 9, 10, 11, 12, 13, 14, 15, 17, 18, 24, 25

March	2, 3, 9, 10, 16, 17, 18, 23, 24, 29, 30, 31
April	5, 6, 7, 13, 14, 19, 20, 21, 26, 27,
May	2, 3, 4, 10, 11, 17, 18, 23, 24, 30, 31
June	6, 7, 8, 13, 14, 19, 20, 21, 26, 27, 28
July	4, 5, 10, 11, 12, 17, 18, 23, 24, 25, 31
August	1, 7, 8, 13, 14, 20, 21, 27, 28, 29
September	3, 4, 9, 10, 16, 17, 23, 24, 25
October	1, 2, 7, 8, 13, 14, 15, 21, 22, 28, 29
November	3, 4, 10, 11, 17, 18, 24, 25
December	1, 2, 7, 8, 14, 15, 16, 21, 22, 23, 24, 29

Spending

It's always fun to spend but the following dates are more in tune with this activity and are likely to give you better results:

January	3, 4, 5, 6, 7, 8, 9, 10, 11, 12, 13, 14
February	3, 4, 5, 10, 19
March	8, 10, 11, 13, 14, 19
April	7, 8, 11, 12, 22
May	6, 7, 8, 9, 10, 11, 12, 13, 17, 18, 19, 20, 21, 22, 23, 24, 25, 26, 27, 28
June	1, 11, 12, 14, 16, 17, 19, 23, 25, 26, 27, 28, 29, 30
July	6, 7, 8, 23, 24, 25, 26, 27, 28, 29, 31
August	1, 2, 3, 4, 5, 15, 16, 17, 18, 19, 30, 31
September	1, 2, 3, 4, 17, 18, 19, 20, 21, 22, 23, 27, 28, 29, 30

October	4, 7, 12, 13, 14, 15, 16, 17, 18, 19, 27, 28
November	2, 3, 4, 25, 26, 27, 28
December	11, 22, 23

Selling

If you're thinking of selling something, whether it is small or large, consider the following dates as ideal times to do so:

January	18
February	12, 13, 14, 15
March	5, 6, 9, 14, 15, 16, 17, 18, 19, 21
April	1, 3, 4, 5, 22, 26
May	7, 12, 21, 29
June	3, 8, 9, 10, 11, 12, 13, 17, 24, 25, 26, 27, 28, 30
July	1, 2, 7, 9, 10, 11, 25, 27, 28, 29, 30, 31
August	1, 2, 3, 4, 5, 6, 7, 8, 9, 10, 13, 20, 23, 28
September	2, 9, 10, 11, 12, 13, 14, 15, 16, 17, 18, 19, 20, 21, 22, 23, 24, 26, 30
October	1, 2, 3, 4, 6, 7, 10, 11, 17, 18, 19, 20, 21, 22, 23, 24, 25, 27, 29
November	3, 4, 5, 6, 7, 11, 14, 15, 16, 17, 18, 19, 21, 23, 24, 25, 26, 27, 28, 29, 30
December	1, 2, 3, 4, 5, 6, 7, 8, 9, 10, 11, 12, 13, 14, 15, 16, 17, 18, 19, 20, 21, 22

Borrowing

Few of us like to borrow money, but if you must, taking out a loan on the following dates will be positive:

January	12, 30
February	7, 12, 13
March	6, 7, 8, 11
April	3, 4, 8
May	9, 28, 29
June	1, 2, 3, 4, 5, 29, 30
July	1, 2, 3, 26, 27, 28, 29, 30
August	9, 25, 26
September	5, 6
October	3, 30
November	26, 27
December	3, 4, 21, 22, 23, 30, 31

Work and education

Your career is important, and continual improvement of your skills is therefore also crucial professionally, mentally and socially. The dates below will help you find out the most appropriate times to improve your professional talents and commence new work or education associated with your work.

You may need to decide when to start learning a new skill, when to ask for a promotion, and even when to make an important career change. Here are the days when your mental and educational power is strong.

Learning new skills

Educational pursuits are lucky and bring good results on the following dates:

January	15, 16, 17, 18, 19, 20, 21, 22, 25, 26, 27
February	14, 15, 16, 17, 18, 19, 22, 23, 28
March	16, 17, 18, 21, 22, 27, 28
April	17, 18, 24, 25
May	15, 16, 21, 22
June	12, 17, 18, 24, 25
July	15, 16, 21, 22, 23, 24, 25
August	11, 12, 17, 18, 19
September	8, 13, 15, 20, 21, 22
October	11, 12
November	7, 8, 9
December	6, 19, 20

Changing career path or profession

If you're feeling stuck and need to move into a new professional activity, changing jobs could be done at these times:

January	6, 7, 15, 16, 17, 23, 24
February	12, 13, 14, 19, 20, 21
March	19, 20, 27, 28
April	15, 16, 24, 25
May	14, 21, 22
June	17, 18, 19, 20, 21
July	8, 9, 15, 16, 23, 24, 25

August	5, 6, 11, 12, 20, 21, 22, 23
September	1, 2, 8, 13, 14, 15, 17
October	8, 13, 14, 15, 16, 17
November	3, 4, 10, 11, 19, 20, 21
December	1, 2, 3, 7, 8, 17, 18, 28, 29

Promotion, professional focus and hard work

To increase your mental focus and achieve good results from the work you do; promotions are also likely on these dates:

January	4, 5, 6, 11, 12, 13, 14, 15, 16, 17, 18, 19, 21
February	6
March	16, 17, 18, 19, 20, 21, 23, 24, 25, 26, 27, 28, 29
April	8, 28, 29
May	12, 21
June	25, 26, 27, 28
July	4, 5, 8, 9, 12, 13, 14, 15, 16, 17, 18, 19, 20, 21, 22, 23, 24, 25, 26, 27
August	5, 6, 10, 11, 12, 13, 14, 15, 16, 17, 18, 19, 20, 21, 22, 23, 24
September	13, 14, 15
October	10, 11, 12, 13, 14, 15, 17, 18, 19, 20, 22, 23, 24, 30, 31
November	2, 4, 5, 6, 7, 8, 9, 23, 24, 25, 26, 27, 28, 29, 30
December	2, 3, 4, 11, 12, 13, 14, 15, 16, 18, 19, 20, 21, 23, 24, 25

Travel

Setting out on a holiday or adventurous journey is exciting. Here are the most favourable times for doing this. Travel on the following dates is likely to give you a sense of fulfilment:

January	15
February	15, 16, 18, 19, 20, 21
March	16, 17, 18, 21, 22, 23
April	19, 24, 25, 26, 27
May	16, 17, 18, 21, 22
June	17, 18, 19, 20, 21, 24, 25
July	21, 22, 23, 24, 25
August	19
September	9, 21, 22
October	18, 19, 20, 21, 22
November	7, 16, 17, 18
December	6, 14, 16, 19, 20

Beauty and grooming

Believe it or not, cutting your hair or nails has a powerful effect on your body's electromagnetic energy. If you cut your hair or nails at the wrong time of the month, you can reduce your level of vitality significantly. Use these dates to ensure you optimise your energy levels by staying in tune with the stars.

Hair and nails

January	1, 2, 3, 4, 5, 6, 7, 8, 11, 12, 13, 14, 15, 18, 19, 20, 21, 22, 25, 26, 27
February	3, 4, 5, 7, 8, 15, 16, 17, 18, 19, 22, 23, 24, 25
March	2, 3, 4, 6, 7, 8, 14, 15, 21, 22
April	1, 2, 3, 4, 5, 10, 11, 12, 17, 18, 19, 20, 21, 22, 23, 28, 29, 30
May	1, 2, 3, 4, 5, 7, 8, 9, 10, 11, 12, 13, 15, 16, 17, 18, 25, 26 27, 28, 29, 30
June	4, 5, 11, 12, 14, 15, 16, 24, 25
July	1, 2, 3, 8, 9, 12, 13, 14, 21, 22, 28, 29, 30
August	1, 2, 5, 6, 17, 18, 19, 25, 26
September	1, 2, 6, 7, 14, 15, 21, 22, 23, 24, 28, 29, 30
October	3, 4, 11, 12, 18, 19, 20, 25, 26, 27, 28, 29, 30
November	7, 8, 9, 14, 15, 16, 22, 23, 24, 25, 26, 27
December	5, 6, 12, 13, 19, 20, 21, 22, 23, 24, 25

Therapies, massage and self-pampering

January	6, 7, 13, 14, 15, 18, 19, 20, 21
February	2, 3, 9, 11, 14
March	1, 9, 14, 16, 17, 20, 23, 29
April	4, 5, 6, 10, 11, 12, 13, 17, 25, 26
May	2, 3, 7, 8, 9, 10, 11, 14, 15, 16, 17, 22, 23, 24, 31
June	3, 5, 12, 18, 19, 26, 27
July	4, 7, 8, 9, 10, 16, 23, 28, 29, 30, 31
August	3, 4, 5, 6, 7, 13, 20, 21, 24, 25, 26, 27, 28, 31
September	2, 17, 21, 28, 29

October	13, 14, 15, 18, 19, 21, 25, 26, 27, 28
November	2, 3, 9, 11, 14, 15, 16, 17, 21, 24, 29
December	7, 12, 13, 14, 15, 18, 19, 20, 22, 26, 27, 28, 29

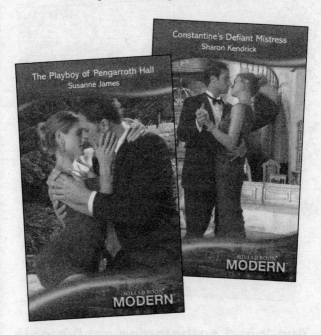

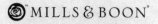

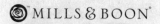

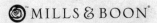

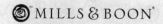

millsandboon.co.uk Community

Join Us!

The Community is the perfect place to meet and chat to kindred spirits who love books and reading as much as you do, but it's also the place to:

- ■ Get the inside scoop from authors about their latest books
- ■ Learn how to write a romance book with advice from our editors
- ■ Help us to continue publishing the best in women's fiction
- ■ Share your thoughts on the books we publish
- ■ Befriend other users

Forums: Interact with each other as well as authors, editors and a whole host of other users worldwide.

Blogs: Every registered community member has their own blog to tell the world what they're up to and what's on their mind.

Book Challenge: We're aiming to read 5,000 books and have joined forces with The Reading Agency in our inaugural Book Challenge.

Profile Page: Showcase yourself and keep a record of your recent community activity.

Social Networking: We've added buttons at the end of every post to share via digg, Facebook, Google, Yahoo, technorati and de.licio.us.

www.millsandboon.co.uk

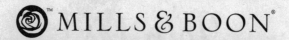